ELVIS
MY DAD

THE UNAUTHORIZED BIOGRAPHY OF LISA MARIE PRESLEY

BY
DAVID ADLER
AND
ERNEST ANDREWS

A 2M COMMUNICATIONS LTD. PRODUCTION

ST. MARTIN'S PAPERBACKS

ELVIS, MY DAD: THE UNAUTHORIZED BIOGRAPHY OF LISA MARIE PRESLEY

Copyright © 1990 by David Adler and Ernest Andrews and 2M Communications Ltd.

Photo research by Amanda Rubin.

ISBN: 0-312-92197-7

Printed in the United States of America

St. Martin's Paperbacks edition/August 1990

10 9 8 7 6 5 4 3 2 1

A CONQUERING LOVE AND THE DAWN OF A ROYAL DYNASTY

Priscilla's pregnancy tightened the bond between mother and daughter. They attended Lamaze classes together and Lisa was present at the birth of her half-brother Navarone, in April of 1986.

Lisa immediately fell in love with her little half-brother. Priscilla was so proud of her new child and her wonderful new relationship with Lisa. It seemed as if the rocky times were far behind them, soon to become only distant memories.

Priscilla must have been so pleased with how her daughter's life was proceeding: Lisa was a devout Scientologist, involved in a stable relationship with a young man who loved her and treated her right, free from drugs, and finally at peace with her father's legacy. Lisa was the very emblem of someone who was in control of her life.

Then one day, Lisa made an announcement to her mother that took Priscilla completely by surprise.

"Mom, you know, I'm pregnant."

ACKNOWLEDGMENTS

We would like to thank the following people without whose support this book would not have been possible.

The Baroness Alina Morini for her invaluable advice and assistance.

The entire staff of American Masters—Harlene Freezer, Diane Dufault, Chris Benjaminsen, and Susan Lacy—for their unflagging enthusiasm, their editorial input, and most of all, for forcing us to go deeper.

Faith Popcorn.

Helen Cutting Whitney and Benno C. Schmidt for their belief in us and this project.

Madeleine and Amanda for their professionalism.

The libraries of Harvard and Yale, and the Lincoln Center for the Performing Arts Archives.

Sarah Nix, our Memphis researcher, and Stuart Patterson, our liaison at the Library of Congress.

The Barnes family of Memphis for their hospitality during our many months of research.

All those interviewed in Memphis, Beverly Hills, Vegas, New York, Graceland, and even as far afield as South Korea, for their time and honesty. Due to the controversial nature of some of these interviews, we have honored their request not to be mentioned by name.

And above all else, we would like to thank Lisa Marie Presley Keough, whose courage, perseverance, integrity, and attitude provided a constant source of inspiration. Thank you, Lisa.

My love for my dad . . . is only for my dad
—not [because he was] Elvis Presley.
—Lisa Marie Presley

She's the only child I have and she's more
precious to me than my life.
—Elvis Presley

PROLOGUE

The King Is Dead

★————————————————————★

2:10 P.M.
August 16, 1977

"MY DADDY'S DEAD, MY DADDY'S DEAD!"

Lisa Marie Presley ran through the halls of Graceland, tears streaming down her face.

First she flew up the stairs to her room, then she suddenly darted in the other direction, down the stairs and into the kitchen. Then back to her bedroom. Lisa ran on and on. Grandma

★

Presley, now in her eighties, tried desperately to hold Lisa in order to calm her but could not assuage her. She was inconsolable and in a frenzy. But her running was pointless, for upstairs was a tragedy from which she could not run away.

Minutes before, Elvis' girlfriend, Ginger Alden, had awakened to find Elvis missing from their bed. She was not immediately concerned until she strolled into their bathroom and saw him lying facedown on the bathroom floor.

His face was discolored. It was grotesque, swollen and purplish. His engorged tongue was clenched between his teeth. He barely resembled the heartthrob and teen idol he had been.

Alarmed, but not yet hysterical, Ginger telephoned for help. Members of the Graceland staff came running. They turned Elvis over and began administering mouth-to-mouth resuscitation.

Their panic intensified. Nothing was working. They called for medical help. From the start of the commotion, nine-year-old Lisa had known something was very wrong. She had heard the noises and cries coming from her daddy's room.

Lisa approached the source of the noise.

Soon the medical help arrived. They would pump air into Elvis' lungs. Later they would inject stimulants in an attempt to revive him and

★

use electrodes to try to shock his body back into action.

Lisa reached the bedroom door.

She was met by Ginger who struggled to keep her away.

"What's wrong with my daddy?" Lisa yelled.

Ginger blocked her way. "There's nothing wrong, Lisa," she replied. Ginger quickly shut the door.

But Lisa wasn't fooled. "Something's wrong with Daddy and I'm going to find out."

She darted to the other door to the room. No one could stop her. This door was still open and Lisa looked inside.

She saw her daddy lying on the bathroom floor. The doctor shouted for Elvis to breathe as Aunt Delta continued mouth-to-mouth resuscitation. Chaos reigned.

Despite all their efforts to revive Elvis, nine-year-old Lisa knew exactly what was wrong. It was too late. Elvis—her daddy—was dead. The body was already cold.

Lisa was alone now. All her life she had played Princess to the King, and now he was dead.

Elvis Presley had been many things to many people: rock star, movie star, sex symbol—in short, the King. But to one nine-year-old girl he

★

was something very different—he was her daddy. And now he was gone.

He would pass on much to Lisa. Graceland would be held in trust for her. She was his only heir, both to his fortune and to his legend. Even then her features bore an uncanny resemblance to his.

Someday, unbelievable as it seemed then, she would start a family of her own. Little Lisa had so much ahead of her. But for the moment all she had was the death of her father.

It was the end of her childhood. But as Elvis' daughter, it was a childhood like no other . . .

★

ONE

A ROYAL BIRTH

★——★

IT WAS A COLD WINTER IN MEMPHIS. SNOW MAY still have been on the ground, but nature's seasonal sleep was about to end. The faintest traces of new blossoms and buds were appearing. New life would soon emerge.

Inside Priscilla Presley, married for only eight months to Elvis Presley, the King of Rock and Roll, a baby stirred. "Any day now," Priscilla must have thought to herself in her final months of pregnancy.

★

Priscilla was barely out of her teens. Her face, despite the adult makeup and hairstyle, was still in some ways that of a child. A child having a child.

Elvis would be returning home soon, home to Graceland. He was finishing up another of his movies, *Speedway,* co-starring Nancy Sinatra.

Priscilla waited nervously for his return. Although the past few months had not been easy ones, Priscilla and Elvis had been living together for six years.

Priscilla had begun dating Elvis when she was fourteen, and moved into Graceland when she was sixteen. In love with this nubile schoolgirl, Elvis transformed her fresh-faced, innocent beauty into something much more glamorous and sophisticated, an effect created by lots of black eyeliner and a towering beehive hairdo, dyed Elvis' own shade of Ultra Black.

After so many years of pleasing Elvis and looking perfect for him, Priscilla's body was now changing. A pregnant wife with a swelling figure, she continually worried if he would still find her attractive.

When she looked in the mirror, she saw that it was hard to tell that she was pregnant. As soon as Priscilla learned that she was going to have a baby, she went on a diet so she wouldn't show. She was determined not to get fat. Although the doctors told her that a weight gain of twenty-

★

five pounds was to be expected, Priscilla was driven to maintain her figure.

She had just one meal a day. The only snack she would allow herself was a hard-boiled egg or an apple. Priscilla even rebelled against the doctor's recommendation to eat more dairy products by eating even less than before she was pregnant.

She dropped from 110 to 100 pounds. By now, in her eighth month, she was only four pounds above her normal weight. She never needed any maternity clothes. Looking in the mirror, she must have taken pleasure that the pregnancy was barely visible.

She had had so many doubts about having this baby. It had happened so soon in their marriage. Priscilla learned she was pregnant only weeks after the wedding. She loved Elvis completely and intended to spend the rest of her life with him, but neither of them had planned to have a child right away. What would this mean for their life together?

At Graceland, before she was pregnant, life had been an around-the-clock party. The kitchen was always open, with cooks on hand twenty-four hours a day to provide down-home favorites. Elvis would spend money lavishly on whatever whim pleased him. They did what they wanted, whether that meant staying up till six A.M., taking off to Vegas at a moment's no-

★

tice, or racing around the estate on go-carts. Were these carefree days gone for good?

Early in her pregnancy, overwhelmed by these doubts and uncertainties, Priscilla had considered her ultimate option. Although Elvis was thrilled with the possibility that he might become a father, he was aware of the fears and reservations of his young wife.

He took Priscilla aside and looked deeply into her eyes.

"What do you want to do, little one?"

Priscilla then understood. Elvis was talking about an abortion. He was letting her make the choice.

"It's our baby," Priscilla said, crying. "I could never live with myself, neither could you."

They made their decision. The Presley name would live on. The infant that was growing inside Priscilla was spared.

Now, months later, as the actual birth approached, the thought of an abortion seemed so far away. Priscilla had accepted the child within her, but was still anxious about her future with Elvis. He was due home any day now.

It was nearly Christmastime at Graceland. Although it was only the first week in December, the blue Christmas lights that Elvis loved decorated the long, winding driveway. There were decorations everywhere and the curtains in the formal living room had been changed to red ones.

On December seventh, Elvis would arrive home. To the world, Elvis Presley was the embodiment of a rock star with an unbridled, almost dangerous sexuality. This sexual charisma, which had attracted so many millions of fans, would seem to be incompatible with the idea of Elvis as a devoted father and husband.

And in fact, even though Elvis was now married to Priscilla, there were rumors about Elvis and Nancy Sinatra on the set of *Speedway*. The crew noticed their long private lunches in her trailer and their visible physical rapport. Pregnant Priscilla could not help but be concerned.

But on that December day when Elvis arrived at Graceland, all of Priscilla's fears were wiped away. When Elvis looked at his wife, his pale blue eyes revealed the love and tenderness he felt for the woman who carried his child. The King of Rock 'n' Roll was truly in love with Priscilla and was ready for an heir.

Almost immediately upon returning home, he ordered a Fleetwood Cadillac limousine for Priscilla so that she and his child-to-be could be carried in safety and luxury. Priscilla, however, would not be so easily pampered. She continued to ride her horse Domino and her dirt bike until the final days of the pregnancy.

★

Elvis expressed his concern about her activities and insisted that she not strain herself in any way. To this end he even went so far as to limit the number of movies they saw each day. Usually, when they rented out a movie theater late at night, they would see two or three films. Now they would return home early after seeing only one. Elvis, the hell-raising rock 'n' roller, had finally become a gentle and protective husband.

Priscilla and Elvis still had to think long and hard about what they would name their child. Together they settled on two choices selected from a book of baby names. If the child was a boy, they planned to name him John Baron after Elvis' grandfather. Priscilla thought that this was a very masculine-sounding name. If the baby was a girl, she would be called Lisa Marie after Marie Mott—the wife of Elvis' business manager, the Colonel. Priscilla told everyone at the baby shower she had a sure feeling it was going to be a boy.

Nancy Sinatra, who had met Priscilla on the set of *Speedway,* gave her the shower. It was held late that December in the exclusive Whitehaven district of South Memphis, near Graceland. A half-day was declared for the ladies who worked in the mansion so that they too could attend the shower. It was a festive occasion, with the guests bringing many baby gifts.

Nancy served punch, accompanied by nuts, mints, chips, and dips, as well as cupcakes with little baby booties on them.

As the due date drew nearer, life at Graceland became more and more frantic. Preparations had to be made. Every detail had to be thought through. There were legions of curious and potentially intrusive fans outside Graceland's music gates. This was, after all, no ordinary baby.

Elvis and his men devised a plan to keep the fans at bay when the baby was born. A black Cadillac would leave the house first and attract any fans that might want to follow it as it sped to Methodist Hospital. However, Priscilla and Elvis would not be in this car. Instead, they would travel in a blue Cadillac up Route 51 to Baptist Memorial Hospital in downtown Memphis. All of Elvis' family at Graceland was expected to follow and a room next to Priscilla's maternity suite had even been booked for them. All of this to protect and treasure the special moment of the baby's birth.

On the morning of February 1, 1968—exactly nine months to the day since their wedding—Priscilla awoke, knowing that it was time. The bed was wet beneath her. After calling her mother and her doctor, she woke Elvis.

Elvis snapped out of his sleep and immedi-

★

ately enacted the plan, hollering downstairs that the baby was on its way.

He called to Mary Jenkins, Graceland's cook, "Get all those boys ready. 'Cilla is in labor."

The bags were already packed. The boys pulled the limousines in front of the house.

Elvis ran out in front of everyone and jumped in the car. "Let's go, let's go, let's go!" he shouted at the driver.

"But Elvis, you haven't got 'Cilla yet!" Mary Jenkins called out from the front porch.

All the boys laughed. Elvis said to them, "Okay—go back and get 'Cilla then."

Inside the house, Priscilla managed to remain calm despite her excitement. She strolled into the bathroom and did her mascara and hair in her famous teased sixties style. Even in this moment of joyous anticipation, Priscilla was still concerned about her looks.

Outside, the fans had assembled by Graceland's music gate. Like crowds outside the Vatican awaiting the smoke signal that proclaims a new pope has been chosen, the fans looked for any sign of the child's imminent birth.

Then they saw the two cars exiting the estate, one after the other. All of Elvis' careful planning did little good. Able to spot their idol no matter what, the decoy plan didn't fool the crowd. The fans followed Elvis and Priscilla in the blue Cadillac instead of the black decoy.

★

Inside Elvis' limo, confusion reigned. The driver got mixed up as to which hospital was the real hospital and which was part of the decoy plan. Was it Baptist Memorial or Methodist? The two were located near each other on Union Street. Everyone had a differing opinion and a decision had to be made quite quickly. This baby was not going to wait. Fortunately, they arrived at the right hospital, Baptist Memorial— the one shaped in a "V," just like an open bible —but the fans were hot on their heels.

After Priscilla was admitted to the maternity ward, off-duty Memphis policemen were stationed outside her room to keep the waiting fans at bay.

The tension in the air was great. Elvis, the man who could stand with ease on a stage in front of thousands, was visibly nervous. He paced inside the doctor's lounge, slightly shaky, a mass of extra energy and anxious concern. Elvis, a man who never waited for anything, who had the whole world at his beck and call, would have to wait for the birth of his child— this baby was on its own schedule.

In the morning's confusion, Elvis hadn't even had time to dress properly or to shave. He returned home in order to change into more fitting garb in which to greet his wife and child— a baby-blue suit with a navy turtleneck. Though now he looked more like the King, in some ways

★

he looked like any other expectant father—nervous.

Seven hours later, the child who would be known as Lisa Marie Presley entered the world at 5:01 P.M. She was six pounds, fifteen ounces, and she was twenty inches long.

Priscilla had been knocked out by Demerol, so Elvis was the first to know of Lisa's arrival. The obstetrician, Dr. Turman, told Elvis, who was waiting outside the room.

"It's a girl, born nine minutes ago. A perfect little girl. Priscilla is fine. It was a perfectly normal birth."

Elvis could hardly believe it—he was a father! He thanked God, and then called his grandmother, Minnie Mae.

"Dodger [as she was called], we got a little girl."

A call was made to Priscilla's mother in California, but the line was busy.

Wanting to spend this time alone with his new family, Elvis sent his father, Vernon, downstairs to inform the reporters who would in turn inform America.

He entered Priscilla's room. Lisa was held close to Priscilla—a perfect Madonna scene, mother and infant daughter. Elvis kissed Priscilla and approached his child.

Lisa had Elvis' dark hair, festooned with a pink ribbon. He turned to Priscilla and spoke,

★

using the couple's personal loving nicknames and secret expressions:

"Nungen [young one], us has a little baby girl."

"Her knows," Priscilla responded.

As Elvis looked at his child he saw a reflection of himself. He looked into her little half-opened eyes. He gently touched her tiny hands and feet that seemed so small yet so human and distinct. In the delicate face of the child he could find traces of his own strong features. He saw suggestions of his heavy-lidded eyes and full lips. The bond between father and daughter was forged.

All was peaceful for the new family. It was an idyllic moment. No one could have guessed that within ten years Elvis would be dead and within twenty, Lisa would be mothering a child of her own. But for now, away from the press and the crowds outside, the family spent this special moment alone, warmly caressing each other. Their happiness seemed complete and unending.

TWO

HOME TO GRACELAND

★───★

AFTER FIVE DAYS IN THE HOSPITAL, IT WAS TIME
for Priscilla and Elvis to bring the infant Lisa
home to Graceland. As they left Baptist Memorial Hospital, Priscilla, seated in a wheelchair
pushed by Elvis, carried little Lisa wrapped in
swaddling clothes. This modern Madonna
sported a trendy miniskirt and hair teased to re-
markable new heights. To complete the look,
Priscilla wore her trademark batwing double
eyelashes that she had requested special per-

★

mission to wear while still in the maternity ward. Elvis beamed at the sight of his new family.

There could be no doubt that these were two overjoyed parents, in love with their offspring and each other. And their complete devotion to their newborn baby was clear. Elvis' Uncle Vester, reminiscing about this time, writes, "This was probably the happiest of all days in the life of Elvis."

For the moment at least, Elvis' career and Priscilla's personal concerns took second place to something greater—the family they had become. The King, his bride, and their daughter returned down Route 51 to Graceland, their castle.

Graceland—the name was magic throughout the land!

Graceland, the legendary home that was a symbol of Elvis and his incredible success. He had bought it for himself early in his career, when he first began to climb the ladder of success. He had been twenty-two, and to the boy who had grown up in a Tupelo, Mississippi shack it was a mansion beyond anything he had ever dreamed possible.

It was where he had brought the woman who was to become his bride when she was but a teenager, to a fantasy world he created for himself, a world of luxury and fun . . . and now the

★

home to which he brought his newborn daughter.

As the family drove up through the tall music gate decorated with notes and a guitar player, the estate in all its splendor unfolded before them. Slowly, they made their way up the long winding driveway to the mansion with its massive columns.

They were coming home. The house bristled with excitement. The staff was busy completing their final preparations for Lisa's arrival. Everyone was so eager. What would life at Graceland be like now that the King and Priscilla were bringing home a baby?

The staff ran to the door as the limousine drove up. Before anyone else had a chance to inspect the tiny bundle, Elvis and Priscilla brought little Lisa straight to Dodger's room, Lisa's great-grandmother. They laid the tiny infant in her lap.

Dodger, all dressed up as usual, beamed with pride and joy at her great-granddaughter.

Then the friends and employees of Graceland had their chance to see her. "Come on, come on now," said Elvis and Priscilla. "Come on and see her." The staff quietly peeked at the beautiful baby Priscilla was holding.

Elvis must have been so proud to bring Lisa Marie home to such a palace. Each of the eighteen rooms bore his personal signature. To call

★

it boldly decorated is an understatement. The personality of its owner—vibrant and unique—is clearly seen in his house. Everything about it was done Elvis-style: grander and more flamboyant than anyone else's.

Little Lisa, cradled in her mother's arms, passed through the house that she would be raised in. They walked by the living room—a dramatic fantasy, decorated in deep, rich blues with a white sofa fifteen feet long (Elvis had it specially made). The blinds could be automatically opened at the touch of a fingertip, but they were always kept tightly closed. Elvis preferred to control his environment rather than rely on fickle nature to provide the climate he wanted. Luxury and comfort abounded in the atmosphere of opulence that Elvis wanted his family to enjoy.

Off the living room was the music room, which featured blue fringed curtains and French Provincial furniture. It was here that Elvis would enjoy playing heartfelt gospel songs on the piano. Little Lisa would grow up in a house filled with the sounds of music, music made by her famous father. The centerpiece of this room, where so much music sprang forth, was the fabulous piano—plated in real gold—a gift from Priscilla.

On the opposite side of the entrance hall was the dining room. Here Elvis sought a baroque

★

effect, glittery and ornate. The dining room table was covered with a smoked-mirror top, which was reflected by mirrors lining the walls. Overhead hung an enormous crystal chandelier. The elegance Elvis desired in these formal rooms contrasts with the playfulness of the basement rooms, rooms where he and Lisa would someday spend hours together.

But it was the nursery for the newborn infant that was the most important room in the house that day. Elvis and Priscilla proceeded up the stairs to the nursery and placed little Lisa in the room that would be hers and hers alone.

Lisa's room was an act of love. Elvis personally shopped for the stuffed toys, statuettes, and wall hangings that decorated her nursery—a former conference room transformed into the perfect room for a baby. Done in a bold yellow and white color scheme, it was just down the hall from Elvis' own bedroom.

As Lisa grew older, her grandfather Vernon would help redecorate the room. A circular king-size bed with white imitation fur and a canopy would replace her crib. Little Lisa would also have a television set, daybed, chairs, bathroom—all decorated in gold and white, with fur accents. Every convenience would be at her disposal, including even a Formica-topped ice-maker.

* * *

From the start, her life as daughter of the King was different from that of other infants. To begin with, she was not baptized. Many were surprised and critical of this, but Elvis preferred to have his daughter grow up free to choose her religious beliefs on her own. Throughout his life he had a deep desire to probe spiritual matters of all kinds and in often unorthodox ways. Although Elvis was a truly religious man, he could not attend church services because of his great celebrity. The fact that she was not baptized into any one religion yet grew up in an atmosphere of spiritual inquiry would eventually have a great impact on Lisa's life. So many doors would be open to her.

Meanwhile, during her first few weeks, all of Lisa's relatives eagerly welcomed her into the family and to Graceland. Throughout his life, Elvis always kept his family nearby. Vernon, Aunt Delta, Uncle Vester, and Elvis' cousin Patsy all arrived to lovingly dote on Lisa.

The fans were equally attentive. Presents poured in. Although the fans were kept outside Graceland's gates, their countless gifts reached the Presleys. Priscilla was no stranger to the media spotlight and she wanted to protect her daughter from its dangers. More importantly, she was aware of the risks of having a child spoiled by such a life-style.

All the presents Lisa received had to go. They were given to charity.

Priscilla thereby established a pattern of child-rearing in this first week that would continue throughout Lisa's childhood.

Lisa's arrival into their lives made her parents enormously happy. Elvis doted on little Lisa, amazed at the baby he had fathered. He was actively involved in Lisa's care, even personally bringing his wife and child to the pediatrician.

But unlike other ordinary fathers, when Elvis wanted a weekend retreat with his family, they'd take off in a private jet! In fact, when Lisa was only four weeks old, they all took a vacation together in Hawaii. When they got back a few days later, Elvis' staff teased Baby Lisa about her trip. The cook, Mary Jenkins, joked, "Lisa, here I am a hundred years old and you're only four weeks old and you've been to Hawaii!" Everyone laughed. Elvis was very confident in their wonderful future together as a family.

This confidence as a new father and husband gave him the determination to get back on top. After Lisa's birth, there was a new energy and purpose to his life as he became intent on recapturing some of the vitality of his early career. He wanted Lisa to be proud of him.

★

Elvis had been working hard. As in any traditional family, Elvis, the father, was the breadwinner. However, rather than working nine to five, here the father was performing in such movies as *Live a Little, Love a Little; Speedway;* and *Charro,* and recording albums.

Each of his films made money, yet each seemed more poorly constructed and haphazard than the last. They used so little of his talents.

Given his new attitude, he needed a vehicle to show the world that he was still the King of Rock 'n' Roll. The NBC-TV Christmas special of 1968 provided the answer. This special could revitalize his career, which had been flagging after the numerous bland movies.

In it, he never looked better. He was back in top form. He'd slimmed down considerably and gotten himself into shape. Elvis wore his famous skintight black-leather outfit and delivered a sensational performance.

He was every inch the sexy rock 'n' roller as he delivered renditions of "That's All Right, Mama" alongside soulful performances of old ballads. The Christmas special was an incredible hit, capturing the number-one spot in the ratings. Abroad, 92.5 percent of Japanese viewers watching TV were tuned to the show. As the cameras panned the smoldering, leather-clad Elvis' provocative performance you would never guess he was such a devoted family man.

★

But in fact, the rock 'n' roller who cavorted on camera in that holiday special, the one whose real-life escapades and unruly behavior were barely suggested by the special, spent that Christmas quietly at home with his wife and child.

It was Lisa's first Christmas and Elvis made sure to make it special. The entire house was lit up and outside a Nativity scene attracted all of Memphis. The blue drapes in the living room were changed to a rich red. There was a festive Christmas tree with scores of presents underneath. The decorations had gone up right after Thanksgiving and would only come down after Elvis' birthday on the eighth of January. At midnight on Christmas Eve, as was the custom at Graceland, presents were opened. Elvis lavished gifts upon little Lisa. How could she help but be delighted!

But Elvis had one more surprise in store for her. He had his father, Vernon, Lisa's grandfather, dress up as Santa to please her. Little Lisa was surely enraptured by this fairly-tale Christmas. So much was done to make this a special time for her. She was truly the center of attention, the newly arrived star of Elvis' universe.

THREE

Baby Lisa

★──────────────────────────────────────★

LISA'S IDYLLIC CHILDHOOD CONTINUED IN THE same fairy-tale way in which it had begun. To the casual observer, Elvis, Priscilla, and Lisa were a very happy family unit.

For Lisa's first birthday, they decided to take a special trip. As a break from Graceland and a retreat from the pressures of Elvis' film career in California, they went to Aspen. They thought that the mountains, the fresh air, and the snow would be fun for her. Elvis rented a private As-

★

pen ski lodge for his family, where they could spend two weeks together playing with Lisa in the snow. She was a beautiful baby with her blond hair under a snow cap and her cheeks rosy from the cold.

After this vacation, the three of them returned to Graceland where Elvis recorded two gold albums and three million-selling singles. *Billboard* magazine said, "He's never sounded better, and the choice of material is perfect." Elvis the singer was back!

However, all these new recording projects took up a lot of time, meaning time away from Lisa. He and Priscilla were used to such separations, but little Lisa was not. His career called him in one direction, his new family in another. What was he to do?

TV provided the answer, perhaps because he was such a huge media star. He thought up the idea of having Lisa's time apart from him filmed! This way he would not miss a single moment of her growing up. To Elvis' great joy, Priscilla continually sent him videotapes and Polaroids of Lisa. These captured priceless moments of Lisa's childhood. Elvis, now content that he was being a good father, could throw himself into his work.

As Elvis was so busy, Priscilla was responsible for Lisa on a day-to-day basis. At first, although delighted with having a child, Priscil-

★

la's first priority was still Elvis. She still spent hours grooming herself to please him. The demands of being Mrs. Elvis Presley and looking the part took up more time than caring for her daughter. Lisa's care was often left in the hands of a rotating group of nurses. First they tried the German-born Anna Marie, but she was hospitalized after a horrible accident on one of Elvis' vehicles used on Graceland's grounds. Finally, they settled on faithful Henrietta Gibson.

But an incident with baby Lisa permanently changed Priscilla's priorities. The family was going to pose for a picture. Lisa, however, refused to let go of her nurse's hand, indicating that Lisa was more comfortable with the nurse than with her own mother. Priscilla finally bribed her with toys, but the lesson was clear. Mother and daughter needed more time together.

And they spent more time together. Priscilla devised special down-to-earth mother-daughter outings. They would go to nearby parks or for strolls or to the Memphis Zoo in Overton Park. Every day, Lisa and Priscilla would go to the YWCA for swimming lessons, so that Lisa was able to swim before she was even three.

Sometimes Priscilla would take Lisa on trips to the main Memphis department store, Goldsmiths, located on the bluffs above the Mississippi, to buy baby clothes. These activities, along with all of Lisa's most recent developments, were included in the film-and-photo care packages Priscilla continued to dutifully send to Elvis. Priscilla designed all these outings with Lisa to be far more down-to-earth than Elvis' well-meant but wild extravagances.

For example, on Lisa's second birthday, celebrated with Elvis in Las Vegas, Elvis filled an entire penthouse suite with balloons. The gift she received might have been right for Las Vegas but was totally out of line for a two-year-old—her very own slot machine. Still, she must have enjoyed playing with the knob and watching the wheels spin even if she didn't know what it meant.

Since the phenomenal success of his 1968 Christmas special, Elvis was spending more and more time in Las Vegas, away from Priscilla and Lisa. Besides his film commitments, beginning in 1969 Elvis headlined in Vegas for several months a year. It was there that he truly reestablished his legendary status.

The packaged stage shows of Las Vegas could not have been further from Elvis' rebellious youthful performances. He was no longer the dangerous rebel, feared by parents and preachers, but now appealed to these parents themselves. They nightly packed the Vegas showrooms in which Elvis appeared.

The former teen idol who had sent adolescent

girls into fainting spells now had the same effect on the housewives and suburban matrons of Las Vegas audiences.

Elvis thought up a brilliant new act featuring karate which drove the audience wild. Elvis pounced and chopped across the stage in a black mohair karate suit. His frenzied but precise karate kicks punctuated the air, in a spectacular display of virility.

He broke all Vegas records and was paid one hundred thousand dollars per week. Over three thousand people were squeezed into the showroom at the International Hotel in order to accommodate the incredible demand.

But back at home in Memphis that gilded voice that had entertained thousands of women in Vegas was never a more pure instrument of emotion than when he sang lullabies to his daughter. Nor did Elvis ever have so appreciative an audience, whose appreciation was expressed not by hysterical screams and yells but by quickly dropping off to sleep.

Elvis, although working hard in Vegas, found time to spend several vacations with the toddler. He would always be there for the holidays and special occasions like the surprise twenty-fifth birthday party he gave Priscilla in 1970. Lisa was beside herself with laughter as Elvis gave everyone go-cart rides. Although Lisa

★

could not drive, she certainly enjoyed the peach ice cream that was served.

Being a good father became more and more important to Elvis. He would tell Lisa Bible stories and listen to her prayers. But not only would he pray with her, he would answer her prayers! Anything a child could desire and more would be hers, even if it was wildly inappropriate for a toddler.

Lisa was given her own pony before she could walk. Elvis would place her on it and the two would travel around the grounds . . . and even inside the house. Grandmother Minnie Mae was annoyed, but Elvis would do anything to make Lisa smile.

And she in turn would make Elvis smile, sometimes sneaking up on him while he played at the gold piano. And what was even more delightful to him, when she got older, was when Lisa would cock her head just like him, and imitate his gestures while displaying his penetrating stare.

As indulgent as Elvis could be, like any good father he wanted to teach Lisa what he considered to be important values. One day as three-year-old Lisa pushed her baby buggy past him, his heart went out to his little girl. Coincidentally, Janelle McComb, a poet from Elvis' hometown of Tupelo, was visiting at the time.

Janelle remarked that Lisa's birthday would

★

soon be coming up. What was he going to get her?

Rather than another fancy gift, a simple poem was what he wanted for her, one that would teach her certain values. "I would like her to remember, and be remembered, for the lady she will become," Elvis explained, "not for what she'll acquire."

Elvis gestured, taking in all his possessions and his huge house. "All of this is but for a day," he went on. He asked Janelle to capture this sentiment in a poem.

When he saw what Janelle wrote, a poem entitled "The Priceless Gift," he cried. He cried because it moved him so much to be able to impart something more than his wealth to Lisa: his values. By sharing his values, he would mold her into a daughter he could be proud of. Like himself, Elvis wanted her to become a self-directed and generous human being.

Such lines as "Bought treasures go so fast" convey the poem's heartfelt sentiment about the value of love versus material possessions.

Elvis had the poem framed and wrote at the bottom: "This is beautiful! Thank you. Elvis Presley." One can still see where his tears fell on the signature, so moved was he by this "Priceless Gift" to his little girl.

★

FOUR

DADDY'S LITTLE GIRL

★————————————————————————————★

WHEN LISA WAS ONLY ONE AND A HALF, WHILE
Elvis was performing in Vegas, pregnant
Sharon Tate was murdered. The effect on Elvis
was immediate and intense. Instantly, Elvis became obsessed with the safety of his family.
Elvis and Priscilla had recently bought a Los
Angeles home where Lisa was currently staying
with her mother. It was on an isolated cul-de-
sac near the house where in her eighth month
of pregnancy Sharon Tate had been stabbed.

★

Elvis ordered armed, round-the-clock security guards for his family. From now on, whenever Lisa went anywhere, her safety was a factor.

As daughter of the world's most famous entertainer, Lisa was a prime target for kidnapping and extortion. In what could have been a very public childhood, Lisa was kept under cover in an anti-publicity and security effort which continued until her marriage at twenty.

One way Elvis could ensure her safety was to prevent photographers from snapping her photo. If Lisa and Priscilla kept a low profile, rarely appearing in public and remaining somewhat mysterious to the press, perhaps then they might be safe.

One day while they were at their Los Angeles home near the Tate estate, Elvis, Priscilla, and Lisa were lounging by the pool when they heard a clicking sound. Someone was taking pictures of Lisa and the rest of the family. Elvis spotted the intruder on a rocky outcropping above the house. Elvis jumped up from his lounge chair and chased after the man, who immediately fled. The intruder, in his fear, slipped and fell down the hill, scattering his camera equipment everywhere. Neither Elvis nor the bodyguards caught the man or recovered the camera and its negatives. Elvis hoped the film had been exposed during the fall, but to his dismay the pictures appeared shortly thereafter in a tabloid.

★

After this incident, when Lisa's nurse Henrietta Gibson was off duty, he would sometimes ask a bodyguard to sleep in her room. He told a close friend, the karate expert Ed Parker, just how concerned he was. "She's the only child I have, and she's more precious to me than my life."

Lisa's childhood continued in a kingdom of light and beauty, but the first dark shadows had been cast. Although outwardly this toddler was as playful as ever, perhaps she subconsciously detected the fear for her safety that her father had. Her response was, no doubt, to turn even closer to the father who would surely protect her.

Lisa always felt safe in her daddy's arms. Elvis and Lisa's favorite time together was spent driving around the grounds of Graceland in a golf cart, with Lisa sitting on her daddy's lap. They would spend hours playing together this way, just the two of them blissfully cruising over the estate. Elvis was filled with justifiable pride at the way he could take care of his little girl.

Priscilla, equally concerned about Lisa's safety, frowned upon Elvis' extravagances when it came to Lisa. Even before Lisa was born, she said to a secretary at Graceland, "I'm not going to have my baby spoiled by being given everything it wants. If you want to build

★

character you have to teach children that it takes effort to earn the good things."

Priscilla's disciplined, middle-class background made her naturally disapproving of self-indulgence and excess. She was by far the stricter parent, readily admitting to being the disciplinarian. She was openly critical of all the inappropriate gifts Lisa got for her birthdays, like the slot machine.

Even a grandfather's natural impulse to spoil his granddaughter was affected. Vernon had to think twice before giving Lisa a huge doll. "Priscilla doesn't want Lisa spoiled, you know," he confessed nervously.

Against Priscilla's best intentions, Elvis began to introduce Lisa to his life-style. No longer an infant, she was becoming nocturnal, staying up till all hours of the night and sleeping all day.

One weekend when Priscilla left a slightly older Lisa in Elvis' hands, she phoned Elvis after midnight inquiring, "Did she have her bath and is she in bed yet?"

Elvis replied, "Yeah, she's taken care of."

But soon Aunt Delta phoned from Memphis and said that Lisa had not taken her bath and was not asleep. It was well after one A.M. When Priscilla confronted Elvis with what she knew to be the truth, he said, "Ah, let her stay up—it's no big deal."

Elvis quite literally let Lisa run wild. Stories

★

abound of her racing through the mansion, jumping up and down, with Elvis nonchalantly looking on. As soon as she learned how to ride her bike, she was a terror in the house, cruising around the formal dining room table. After all, she was Daddy's little girl. He almost always referred to her by pet nicknames like Yisa and Buttonhead. It's not surprising that according to servants at Graceland, her first word was "Dada." The trouble was, Elvis was rarely ever firm with her, preferring to indulge her.

Elvis found it impossible to raise his voice to her. At most a firm "Lisa" was all he could manage. This reluctance to discipline Daddy's little girl can be seen in countless incidents which might otherwise be dismissed as trivial except for what they reveal about this father-daughter relationship.

At dinner one night young Lisa sat between her parents eating spinach. Except Lisa was not so much eating the spinach as mushing it between her fingers and spreading it all over herself. Elvis, on a visit home from Las Vegas, was a very fussy eater and found Lisa's childish behavior unappealing. He tried to disguise his distaste from Lisa by jokingly saying to the maid, "We'll be eating in the den. Lisa will join us after she's finished playing with her meal." It simply was not in his heart to reprimand her.

Aware of who her father was and that he

★

adored her, but not understanding the consequences of what she was doing, Lisa began to wreak havoc with the staff. If a servant wouldn't do something four-year-old Lisa wanted, Lisa figured out quite cleverly that she could manipulate them.

She would wield her power over them, saying, "I'm gonna tell me daddy and you're going to get fired." The servants, knowing how much Lisa meant to Elvis, often let her get her way.

Priscilla was outraged. What was she learning? Is this what being Elvis' daughter meant? All the promises she'd made to herself about how Lisa would be raised were being undermined by Elvis.

But Lisa's behavior could be corrected in time. She was a little girl with much to learn. Elvis, on the other hand, was more set in his patterns, patterns which threatened to destroy their marriage. As Lisa grew from infant to toddler, her parents, although devoted to her, were growing further and further apart.

FIVE

ARE YOU LONESOME TONIGHT?

★————————————————————★

THE EVENTS WHICH WOULD TEAR YOUNG LISA'S world apart began when she was little more than an infant. Like so many housewives, Priscilla, despite her many servants, must have found caring for an infant without a husband around a strain. While Elvis was living a glamorous Las Vegas life, she was the one who had to calm the crying baby, she was the one who had to take care of Lisa's sniffles and other baby upsets.

★

Sometimes Priscilla got the break she needed and time alone with her husband when Lisa was left with Priscilla's parents, the Beaulieus, in suburban New Jersey.

Captain Joseph P. Beaulieu, Priscilla's father, was a career air force man. He was a strict disciplinarian. Although he allowed his daughter to date Elvis when she was only fourteen, it was only after being impressed by the enlisted Elvis' courteous respect. And it was with much deliberation that he let his daughter move into Graceland at the age of sixteen. (Actually, Priscilla was the Captain's stepdaughter. Priscilla's biological father had been killed in World War II. Priscilla's mother, Ann, married the Captain, who grew to love Priscilla as his own child.)

When they saw their grandchild, the product of Elvis and Priscilla's love, all of Joseph and Ann Beaulieu's past reservations and anxiety about their daughter's relationship with Elvis must have been totally forgotten.

As a military couple they understood the value of discipline. But try as they might, it must have proved difficult not to indulge such a beautiful child. At this early age, Lisa already felt not only the Presleys' love, but also the Beaulieus'.

At other times Lisa would accompany Elvis and Priscilla on their trips. Elvis, Priscilla, and Lisa, needing to spend time together as a fam-

★

ily, attended the Grand Karate Tournament in Hawaii at the beginning of May 1969. Karate was so important to Elvis and it would be exciting to see so many karate stars. Perhaps this family outing would ease the growing strains between husband and wife.

On stage on the first night of her Hawaiian trip, Priscilla saw the karate star who would ultimately come between her and Elvis—Mike Stone. For the moment, Priscilla was still completely faithful to Elvis despite the problems they were having with their marriage, problems caused by the unique situation of being married to Elvis.

Elvis was away so much and she was trapped in his mansion, always waiting for him, always looking perfect for him. Yes, Lisa was a great consolation. But otherwise, she seemed to be living in a gilded cage.

And when Elvis and Priscilla were together, they were almost never alone. Seeing only the same set of friends and bodyguards must have been so wearying. Priscilla had hoped their Hawaiian trip would be the opportunity for a romantic reconciliation—finally, some time where she and Elvis could be together—but even on this "second honeymoon" nine people accompanied them.

Out of the blue, Elvis one day insisted that Priscilla accompany him to Vegas less often.

Priscilla was confused. Why didn't Elvis want her in Vegas? It was always such fun to be there with him. Priscilla must have had her suspicions about what was going on behind her back. She'd no doubt heard about the wild pool parties with the showgirls. Her suspicions were confirmed when she found a love letter to Elvis signed "Miss Lizard Tongue."

But when Elvis was home the real problem in their marriage arose. Unlike the rumors about what was going on in Vegas, the trouble at home could not be ignored.

The simple fact was, Elvis and Priscilla had always had a strange sexual relationship. During the many years they lived together before they were married, Elvis and Priscilla never consummated their love; Elvis would not permit them to take the final step of lovemaking until they were man and wife. Despite this enforced chastity, they had a very intense sexual bond. Although making love in the traditional way was off-limits, Priscilla found ways to please Elvis.

For instance, they would wrestle together with Priscilla wearing only her panties. Or she would wear costumes. She would pretend to be a schoolmistress seducing her naughty student. Or she might dress up in her high school uniform and play the eager young pupil herself.

Like many young couples, they enjoyed videotaping and photographing their erotic fantasies. But Elvis did this, as he did everything, on a grand scale. Priscilla would be sent out in the middle of the night, in a ridiculous "disguise," to purchase a dozen packs of Polaroid film. All these efforts to keep Priscilla, the woman he intended to marry and who would someday bear his child, untouched. It was only on their wedding night that Elvis finally allowed their love to be consummated.

The wedding itself had been the embodiment of the glamour of Las Vegas: an exaggerated hairdo and heavy makeup for Priscilla, upswept hair and tuxedo for Elvis. In a private ceremony at the Aladdin Hotel, Elvis and Priscilla exchanged vows in front of Judge Zenoff. They were now man and wife.

At last Priscilla could experience the true fulfillment of their love. They drove to their Palm Springs rented home and Elvis carried his virgin bride across the threshold, singing the beautiful "Hawaiian Wedding Song."

They had known each other so well, so intimately, but there had always been restrictions and limits. They had indulged in so many games, so many voyeuristic activities with various sexual toys. Now nothing held them back.

The woman who can tell us best what happens next is the woman who was there—Priscilla Presley.

★

In her own words, Priscilla writes in *Elvis and Me*:

> The desire and lust that had built up in me throughout the years exploded in a frenzy of passion . . . As I went from child to woman, the long, romantic, yet frustrating adventure that Elvis and I had shared all seemed worthwhile. As old-fashioned as it might sound, we were now one.

Although Elvis and Priscilla could not possibly have known it at the time, in nine short months, they would be three.

Lisa's birth changed Elvis' sexual relationship with Priscilla yet again.

The passion that Priscilla and Elvis shared on their wedding night was not to last. After she became a mother, Elvis lost all sexual desire for Priscilla.

Priscilla tried everything. She would cozy up to him in bed, wearing the skimpiest of negligees or appear in Vegas in a see-through dress. She looked fabulous as always, thin and meticulously groomed the way he preferred. But it was to no avail. Try as she might, Priscilla—one of the most beautiful women in the world—seemed to hold no sexual appeal for her once-passionate husband.

The situation was a classic one, as old as Oed-

★

ipus. Once his wife became a mother, Elvis viewed Priscilla as a maternal figure, rather than as a sexual object. His sexual desire for Priscilla was blocked by his new conception of her.

Elvis had been exceedingly close to his mother, Gladys. Until he reached puberty, they even slept in the same bed. Elvis was the most important thing in her life and she smothered him with affection. She led him to school and then home every day, never letting him out of her sight. He was kept away from other children, raised in seclusion with Gladys.

Even though the Presleys were poverty-stricken, Gladys somehow found the money to lavish gifts on Elvis—bicycles and guitars. They even had a private language they shared with one another, used to such a degree that strangers had trouble understanding them. Instead of calling Gladys "Mother," Elvis created a pet name for her, Satnin. He was, in short, a mama's boy.

As someone so remarkably close to his mother, Elvis was unsettled by having a wife bear a child. It permanently shifted his perception of Priscilla from a lover to a mother, stifling all sexual desire. Revealingly, one of Elvis' pet names for Priscilla was Satnin, a name originally reserved for Gladys.

For Priscilla the pain of the situation must

★

have been great. She recognized the cause of the problem but could do nothing about it. In this case, psychological understanding did not lead to a solution.

Priscilla was still young and beautiful, but suddenly Elvis did not desire her. She faced a life without the possibility of sexual love from her husband. Despite having everything that money could buy, she was trapped in a maternal fantasy imposed on her by Elvis.

Of course Priscilla was a mother and of course she loved Lisa, but for her this was not incompatible with having a sexual relationship with her husband. For Elvis, it was. He had trouble accepting Priscilla as his lover and Priscilla as Lisa's mother. Sexual partner or mother of his daughter: he had to choose between the two. And he loved his daughter.

In many ways, he had had a father-daughter relationship with Priscilla, whom he molded and shaped into his feminine ideal. He had begun dating her when she was fourteen, a mere child really. He was so much older and more experienced than the innocent schoolgirl he doted upon. As Priscilla remembers, "As long as I stayed with him I could never be anything but his little girl."

Once Lisa was born, Priscilla could no longer play this role. But Lisa could. She was literally "Daddy's Little Girl" and Elvis loved to indulge

★

her and dote upon her. Later on she would accompany him to concerts instead of Priscilla.

Now Elvis truly could be a father—with Lisa, his daughter, instead of Priscilla, his wife. Lisa soaked up all of his pure paternal affection, leaving little room for sexual feelings for Priscilla. Priscilla, as a mature woman, could not be satisfied with this arrangement, as she had adult needs of her own. She had to get out.

A friendship with the young karate instructor Mike Stone, whom she had met on the Hawaiian trip in 1969, gradually turned into an affair. Despite her love for the father of her child, Priscilla had to break free.

SIX

SEPARATE WAYS

★————————————————————★

FOR A TIME, TO SPARE LISA ANY PAIN, PRISCILLA and Elvis tried to disguise the tensions between them. At Christmas in 1971, when Lisa was almost four, they pretend to be a happy couple as they exchanged gifts and celebrated under the twinkling blue lights of Graceland.

But at the annual Graceland Christmas party, their troubled relationship was plainly apparent. They could no longer hide it from their family and friends.

★

Priscilla was behaving oddly at the party. Everyone could sense the anger coming from her. She smiled to herself as though she were enjoying a private joke. In the corner of the room, away from Elvis, she hinted openly that she was having an affair.

Elvis didn't know what to do with Priscilla. He was beside himself and began drinking, something he very rarely did. Clearly there was trouble in the air. You could cut the tension between them with a knife.

Lisa was caught in the middle. She loved both her parents and wanted them to be happy with each other. Even though she was shielded from the actual outbursts, any bitterness between her parents would ultimately have to hurt her.

The morning after the party Priscilla made her move. Without Elvis, she took Lisa and quietly left Graceland for the house in L.A. Although Elvis wasn't aware of it, Priscilla was intending to leave for good.

She avoided telling Elvis her decision right away. Eventually, she flew out to Vegas and confronted him. She told him she was leaving. Elvis was shocked.

"Are you out of your mind? You have everything any woman could want. You can't mean that, Satnin [his pet name for his dead mother and now for Priscilla]. Goddamn!"

Priscilla did not mention her infidelity. She

★

spared him that, leading him to believe that their marriage was not working out because they were growing apart.

Immediately after telling Elvis, she felt free to move in with Mike Stone, the karate instructor she had been seeing. Packing all her belongings into a station wagon with little Lisa, she set off from the Bel Air estate for the ride to Mike Stone's tiny apartment in Belmont Shores, south of L.A.

On that wintry February day in California, Lisa sat in the car, crammed between boxes and suitcases. She was losing her daddy and heading off for a minute apartment with a strange man.

The next months in her new home must have been difficult for Lisa. She, Priscilla, and Mike moved into a modest two-bedroom apartment in the swinging singles community of Marina Del Rey. How different from Graceland where there were so many servants to wait on her. There old Mary Jenkins would be in the kitchen, ready to cook up her favorite: hot dogs and french fries. And if Lisa wouldn't eat, the staff would put her food on a tray and carry it up to her father's room. Lisa would snuggle into bed next to Elvis, and only then devour the hot dogs she loved so much. Everything at Graceland was cozy and secure—it was home.

Priscilla and Mike did everything to make

★

this time easier for Lisa. They did their best to maintain the positive image that Lisa held of her father, and hide from her the difficulties that he and Priscilla had faced.

But Lisa was a sensitive child. Her dreamy expression often belied the turmoil within. At times there was a sad look in her eyes that didn't used to be there. Lisa wanted her parents back together and Lisa was used to getting what she wanted.

Elvis and Priscilla made the separation official in the summer of 1972. Elvis began to disintegrate. His stepmother, Dee, remembers, "After he and 'Cilla split up he lost control." Drugs, always a part of Elvis' life, became more important than ever.

When Lisa saw him next, in August 1972, he had changed. He seemed slower, sadder. Lisa had flown up to Vegas with her mother and had so looked forward to seeing him. But the look of pain in his eyes, especially when she said good-bye, could not have escaped the notice of even a four-year-old, especially a sensitive one.

Elvis' mood was best reflected in one of the songs he was singing then: "Separate Ways." This was a dramatic change from the blander music he had been recording in the sixties. Elvis was now looking inside himself and the pain was there for everyone to see. The song "Separate Ways" allowed Elvis to pour out his

★

personal torment, as it told the story of a family breaking up.

After Lisa's visit things got even worse. Before, he had always taken downers and sleeping pills to counteract the stress of performing. But now he began taking Dilaudid, an incredibly powerful painkiller given to cancer patients and victims of deep stab wounds. Try as he might to medicate his pain, he could not heal the emotional anguish he was suffering.

He managed to get his act together in time for Lisa's fifth birthday. As usual, she celebrated it with Elvis. Both parents made the effort to be together for this occasion: Priscilla and Lisa flew into Vegas on the morning of Lisa's birthday, and went straight to the Hilton where Elvis was appearing.

The birthday party was held in the Hilton's penthouse, which was specially decorated with balloons and ribbons. There were five pink candles on her cake. Helping Lisa celebrate were Priscilla's friend Joanie Esposito and one of her daughters, Cindy. Elvis was there with his current girlfriend, Linda Thompson. Despite the emotional complications of the day, all attention was focused on Lisa.

During the party, Priscilla and Elvis conferred about Lisa and their separation. When they returned to the table where Lisa was eating

★

cake, Lisa beamed at her parents, happy to see them together again.

She asked hopefully, "Didn't you make things all right, Daddy, so that we can be back together again?"

Elvis was dumbfounded. He had no response for little Lisa's innocent inquiry that expressed a very real need. Priscilla, flustered, reacted by telling Lisa that they would soon have to fly back to L.A.

Lisa's hopes were dashed. "But the party just started," she complained. Things were not turning out the way she had wanted.

Elvis tried to contain his emotions and put up a strong front for his wife and child's benefit. "Do what your mama says," he told her, although he was equally sad that she would be leaving soon.

As his emotions stirred inside him, he spontaneously picked Lisa up, hugging her and lifting her out of her seat.

"Daddy, you made me drop the piece of cake on the floor," she immediately responded.

Lisa did not understand Elvis' impulsive action and the unexpressed feelings that lay behind it.

Elvis, wounded and saddened by Lisa, said, "I'm sorry, honey. I'll get you another cake tomorrow." What else could he say? The party was almost over.

★

Before Priscilla took her away, Lisa caught his stage show at eight P.M. Elvis shone onstage for her as always, belting out many of his early rock songs along with recent hits like "Burning Love" and "Can't Help Falling in Love." But despite his efforts to make this a happy birthday, it turned out to be saddening for father and daughter alike.

When it came time for the midnight show after Lisa had left Vegas, Elvis found he couldn't go on. He couldn't go on the next night either. He had been sick, but this went beyond any illness. Something was very wrong with Elvis. It was as if he'd now lost a part of himself, a part he desperately needed—his wife and his child.

Two weeks later, on February 19, 1973, at three A.M., Elvis lay in his massive bed in the Hilton penthouse. Eyes were narrowed, sweat trickled out of his pores. His rage was seething within him, directed at the man who now had Priscilla and Lisa—Mike Stone. Monotonously, over and over again he repeated the lines to his bodyguards, "The man has to die. You know the man has to die, the sonofabitch must go. There is too much pain in me and he did it. Do you hear me? I am right. You know I am right . . . He must die . . . He has hurt me so much . . . He has broken up my family. He must die. Mike Stone must die."

Apparently, Priscilla had told Elvis that Mike

★

Stone thought it would be good if Lisa didn't visit Elvis for a while. Elvis, his heart already broken by having his wife taken from him, would not allow his daughter to be taken too.

Priscilla may have actually been the one who wanted Elvis away from Lisa because of his increasing drug problems. Priscilla knew in her heart that Elvis was a good father, but she must have been reluctant to expose her daughter to him during his less attractive moments.

But Elvis was provoked by something else too. He had heard a story first circulated by Priscilla's household help. Lisa had been sleeping in the same room, in fact at the foot of the very bed that Priscilla shared with her lover, Mike Stone. This was the final humiliation for Elvis, something that simply could not be tolerated.

Although this rumor was probably false, Elvis believed it and he was enraged. His bodyguards did not know what to do. They had seen their boss in all kinds of moods, but this was different. He seemed to have lost all control as he stomped around the penthouse with an M16 automatic in his hands. He seemed to mean what he said—he really did want Mike Stone dead.

They called Elvis' doctor and tried medicating the ranting King. But when he awoke the next day he continued to issue the order.

Eventually, to placate him, one of the guards got in touch with a Mafia hit man.

★

On the last night of his Vegas show, twenty minutes before Elvis was to go onstage, his bodyguard Red West approached him. West was quite nervous and wary as he told his boss he had found a man for the job. Who knew what Elvis would do? Would he really want to go through with it? Was his love for his daughter and wife this destructive?

Fortunately, Elvis had come to his senses. He paused to swallow the information.

"Aw, hell. Just let's leave it . . . maybe it's a bit heavy."

Red West breathed a sigh of relief. Despite his grief, Elvis had realized that he could not take another man's life, even if that man had taken his wife and daughter. It wasn't right. How would he ever explain it to Priscilla, and more importantly, to Lisa?

He had managed to stop one destructive impulse. But that night he turned his rage inward. Elvis overdosed on Dilaudid and nearly died.

The atmosphere at Priscilla and Mike's apartment was increasingly paranoid. Elvis had been making death threats for over a year. Although they were not aware of the hit-man episode, Elvis' other threats were terrorizing them. He would call and sadistically tell Priscilla that he was coming over with his men and an M16 automatic. He would rant and rave about how he

★

was going to make Mike Stone crawl across the floor in front of Priscilla and then kill him.

Of course, Priscilla tried to keep these threats from Lisa. But the intense fear in Priscilla must have been communicated to Lisa. A child already raised under constant vigilance because of the continuous threat of kidnapping was plunged into an atmosphere of even greater paranoia. Priscilla would try to maintain a cheerful smile, but when the calls came her voice would crack and color would drain from her face while Mike Stone started shouting back. The intense anxiety could only add to Lisa's state of bewilderment and trauma.

Every night little Lisa would pray that things could be like they were . . . that Mommy and Daddy would be together again and they would be a family once more.

Priscilla knew that this period had to end and the only way to end it was to give Elvis more time with his daughter. The only solution was a divorce settlement with mutually acceptable terms regarding Lisa. And perhaps the divorce would stabilize things and settle some of Lisa's confusion and anxieties.

Elvis also needed this finalized divorce settlement, one that would give him open access to his daughter. Any amount of money was worth it.

His performances, although still making

★

money, were receiving mixed, even negative, critical responses. In reviewing his Sahara Tahoe act of 1973, *Variety* reported that:

> Elvis is neither looking nor sounding good. Some 30 pounds overweight, he's puffy, white faced and blinking against the light. The voice sounds weak, delivery is flabby with . . . great effort and no enthusiasm.

What had happened to the master showman? He could no longer hide the chaos of his personal life. The loss of the wife and daughter who had meant so much nearly destroyed Elvis the man and was now dragging down Elvis the performer.

The necessary settlement was at last reached. Priscilla calculated what she needed for herself and Lisa. She presented a list of monthly expenses to the Los Angeles Superior Court:

Clothing	$2,500
Child Care	500
Telephone	400
Entertainment	500
School	300
Rent or mortgage on residence	700
Property insurance and taxes on home	100
Maintenance of residence	500
Food and household supplies	1,000

★

Utilities	150
Laundry and cleaning	300
Medical	200
Insurance (life, health, etc.)	300
Incidentals	1,500
Transportation	1,000
Auto expenses (gas, repair, etc.)	500
Installment payments	1,350

The grand total for these monthly expenses, plus an additional sum for furnishings, was $14,900.

Priscilla was awarded $750,000 in cash, monthly payments of $6,000 for a total of $1,250,000, as well as $1,200 a month alimony for a year. She also received music stock and half the proceeds from the sale of the Holmby Hills estate valued at $500,000. She now had more than enough for herself, her clothes, and her child. Despite this expensive settlement, Elvis profited, for there was one thing that made it all worthwhile—Lisa Marie. Although Lisa would continue to live with her mother, Elvis had joint custody of her.

Elvis and Priscilla left the California court after the divorce was finalized arm in arm. Elvis kissed her and speedily departed in one of his cars. His aim had been accomplished and the tensions with Priscilla could finally be resolved. Most importantly, at her birthday and at Christ-

★

mas, Lisa was his again. Father and daughter could not be separated.

Nothing barred him from Lisa now. There were extended visitation privileges—Lisa and Elvis could continue to spend large amounts of time together, at Graceland and at the openings of all his Las Vegas shows.

He continued his grueling performing schedule. Before Lisa arrived for a Christmas visit he recorded a set of songs at the Stax studios in Memphis. The music from that session reveals the anguish Elvis was feeling, anguish which as an artist he was able to transform into the material of art. He poured forth his suffering into the hits "Good Time Charlie's Got the Blues," "Take Care of Her," and especially "Help Me." Although Lisa would soon be with him and the divorce was over, the choice of these songs reflect the damage that had been done.

When Lisa finally arrived in Memphis for Christmas on December 16, 1973, some things had stayed the same. Mary Jenkins cooked all her favorites. Aunt Delta, Dodger, and her beloved grandfather Vernon were all thrilled to see her. As usual, Elvis showered her with gifts. While gifts were piled up underneath the big tree, most of Lisa's presents were hidden around the house. How she loved to search through the house like a little detective looking for clues.

★

But where formerly there had been stockings for Elvis, Lisa, and Priscilla, now there were stockings for Elvis, Lisa, and Linda. Priscilla's stocking had been replaced by Linda Thompson's, Elvis' new girlfriend.

It was Christmas, but Mommy and Daddy were not together. Yes, she could see her father again, but only too briefly. And Daddy was much sicker. In fact, he had been hospitalized very recently for drug detoxing and for his weight problem. Though he now had his beloved Lisa, he had gone through such emotional extremes to get her, extremes which had taken their toll. Although Lisa was back at Graceland with her father, this Christmas was simply not the same.

SEVEN

THE TINY TERROR

★————————————————————★

IF ELVIS WAS FEELING LOW AFTER THE DIVORCE, Lisa was feeling lower. On her sixth birthday, February 1, 1974, Lisa was hospitalized in Los Angeles because of tonsillitis. Her father had been sick so many times, and now she too knew what it was like to be in the hospital. Elvis was not able to come visit her because of a Vegas engagement. It was her first birthday without him.

But even if he couldn't be with her at this dif-

★

ficult time, he was determined to keep her love. When they were living together, he had always been indulgent. Now as a divorced father, his indulgence knew no bounds.

Of all Elvis' gifts, it was the golf cart that was the most special. Given to Lisa when she was only five and her feet could barely reach the pedals, it instantly became her favorite toy. Lisa's golf cart had her name emblazoned on its side. She and her father would circle the grounds together, laughing happily. At other times, Lisa might take the golf cart out for a spin on her own. Already, she shared her father's love for sporty sets of wheels.

Anything Lisa wanted, Elvis would get for her. When Lisa mentioned she had never seen snow, Elvis sent his jet to transport her to Colorado and then back to L.A. just so she could see some. Once because she looked unhappy, Elvis gave her a diamond smiley pin.

Elvis' wild extravagances contrasted with Priscilla's practical, tightfisted approach to money. At home with Priscilla, when Lisa lost a tooth, she woke up to find fifty cents left by the tooth fairy under her pillow. When visiting Elvis in Vegas, she lost another tooth, but this tooth fairy left a crisp five-dollar bill. Priscilla laughed at this incident, but the drastic differences in Lisa's life-styles at Graceland and in L.A. were growing greater.

★

Priscilla was still adamant that Lisa not be spoiled. She knew firsthand the dangers of Elvis' excesses. When Elvis gave Lisa a white fur coat, Priscilla could see that Elvis meant well, but also saw that it was very inappropriate to give such a gift to a child. Lisa would never wear that coat.

Priscilla continued to stick to her army-brat beliefs and raised Lisa with a firm hand. Lisa's toys were not excessive and she was made to do small chores for a modest allowance. With the divorce settlement, Priscilla and Lisa moved to a larger apartment, but it was still in the same building in Marina Del Rey. This one had three bedrooms. Lisa's life was as close to normal as Priscilla could make it for a child whose father was Elvis Presley.

But this put Priscilla in the unenviable position of so many divorced mothers; they provide discipline and undergo the daily grind of child-raising, whereas Daddy gets to appear as the indulgent Sugar Daddy. And here Daddy was the King, and the indulgences were sky-high.

The bewildering change in environment was taking its toll. Lisa, who had been so sunny and sweet, was developing a new side. No longer a toddler, she was a six-year-old whose personality was developing and clearly expressing itself. Unfortunately, the stresses of her upbringing

★

sometimes showed in moments of unattractive behavior.

When visiting Graceland, the King's daughter was acting increasingly imperious. Snappish and demanding, Lisa was becoming a tiny terror. Phyllis Thompson, a fan from Macon, Georgia, drove to Graceland, hoping to catch a glimpse of Elvis. She climbed a maple tree in order to get a better view. Lisa was out playing in her new golf cart when she spied Phyllis. Lisa strutted over to Phyllis, who was tottering in the tree. "Are you drunk?" Lisa demanded.

Satisfied that Phyllis wasn't, Lisa's inquisition still was not over. "Whose daughter do you think I am?"

Phyllis said that she did not know.

Lisa smugly replied, "Elvis Presley's!"

Phyllis teasingly pretended not to know who he was. "Who is that?" she asked playfully.

"Oh, you know who!" Lisa shouted before scampering back to her golf cart and driving back toward the house.

Clearly Lisa was already aware of who her father was and what this meant.

Her friendships had evolved. Although still close to the children of Elvis' nurse—Deborah and Donna Henley—she had a new close friend in Laura Miller. Laura was the daughter of Vernon's new girlfriend, Sandy. Sandy and Laura lived with Vernon in the house Elvis had

★

bought for him, around the corner from Grace-land.

Lisa would invite Laura to a sleep-over party, but suddenly get angry with her and send her home. But soon after she'd sent Laura packing, Lisa would have a change of heart. She would phone over to Vernon's before Laura got home and demand that she come back. What Lisa wanted, Lisa got, and Laura complied. Because of Lisa's moodiness, the help at Graceland used to joke that little Laura's suitcase should have a set of wheels!

The staff was accustomed to Lisa's demanding nature. The cook recalls Lisa ordering a different cake every day and instructing her, "Don't tell my mother."

Lisa did what she pleased, whether it was staying up till all hours of the night or going where she wanted. When no one was looking she would take the golf cart over the hill behind Graceland where she couldn't be watched. She was clever about these things, finding new ways to get around the rules. As soon as her nurse's back was turned, she would be gone, sneaking around to the pool in back, something she was not allowed to do.

This mischievous behavior extended to meddling in her father's love affairs.

In 1975, Elvis was hot on the heels of Melissa Blackwood, a local Memphis beauty queen who

★

was playing hard to get. Little Lisa decided to interfere. When Elvis was on the phone, wooing Melissa, Lisa would sneak up to the phone and hang up the receiver. She repeatedly disconnected them during Elvis' hour-long conversation.

Elvis would allow her to hang up on him, and would simply redial Melissa's number. Although she was giggling, Lisa's motivations were very serious. She wanted her mommy and daddy together again. Elvis granted all of Lisa's other wishes, but he could not grant this one, he could not get back together with Priscilla.

Perhaps a reunited family was all Lisa really wanted. For even though Lisa may have seemed spoiled and ridiculously overindulged, in some ways she didn't appear to care about material possessions at all.

Witness her response to the biggest material gesture of affection from Elvis—the *Lisa Marie*. In 1975, Elvis spent a million dollars on a blue-and-white passenger jet, formerly owned by Delta Air Lines, for his personal use. However, Elvis was not content with the jet as it was and had to have the interior customized to suit his personal style. At a cost of $750,000 he installed emerald-green shag rugs, a queen-size bed covered with a crushed blue velvet spread, and gold-plated bathroom fixtures. He added a formal dining room that seated eight. For his en-

★

tertainment pleasure, Elvis installed four televisions and also eight telephones in case he needed to make a call.

From now on whenever Lisa traveled to see Elvis, Elvis would send the *Lisa Marie* to pick her up. She slept in her bed in the plane's plush green living room area, right next to Elvis' bedroom. These short, indulgent jet trips became a way of life.

On Lisa's eighth birthday, for example, Elvis was describing to friends the best peanut butter sandwich he'd ever had—found only at the Colorado Mining Company restaurant outside Denver. A whole loaf of bread was slit and smothered with peanut butter and jelly and, to top it all off, a pound of freshly fried bacon. The price was outrageous—$49.50! Elvis raved about these sandwiches. Hungry, they flew to Denver in the *Lisa Marie*, had sandwiches delivered by a limo to the plane, ate them there, and took off —a three-thousand-mile trip at a cost of $16,000.

But the real reason he bought the *Lisa Marie* was neither practical nor self-indulgent. Elvis freely confessed he bought the *Lisa Marie* because "I wanted to impress Lisa." To this end, he even had her name emblazoned in big letters on the plane's nose. But this plane, his biggest gesture of love for Lisa, did not impress her at all. "When I showed it to her," Elvis admitted, "She yawned."

★

Although he risked spoiling Lisa, these indulgences speak of a very real emotional need of Elvis'. Lisa might not have known it, but when Elvis was three he endured a similar separation from his father; Elvis knew firsthand how painful it was not to have a father around all the time because it had also happened to him.

Vernon was taken from his son and wife when he was put in jail for forging a check from the sale of a pig. He needed the money to feed his hungry family. With his father in prison, poor, and ashamed, Elvis grew unbelievably close to his mother, Gladys. The bond between parent and child became all-consuming. The two developed their own private language of pet names as Gladys, although dirt-poor, showered her beloved son with gifts.

The warmth and love that Gladys gave to Elvis when one parent was gone, Elvis now shared with his own child as she was separated from a parent. And as with Elvis and Gladys, the parent-child bond grew incredibly close to compensate for the loss. Hence, Elvis lavished huge gestures of affection on her, such as the *Lisa Marie.* These intense emotions and dramatically different home environments, however, were destined to create a complex, sometimes contradictory, seven-year-old.

Bratty but sweet, lively and energetic but often bored, raised like an heiress but with

★

down-home touches, Lisa's life was a swirling kaleidoscope.

She was a seven-year-old who might run down the Graceland staff in her golf cart and then come to them with her cuts and scrapes. And despite the extravagant toys, one of Lisa's favorite activities was playing on her swing set in the backyard—a simple swing set bought at the five and ten, like any child might have.

However moody, Lisa was also extremely sensitive to those around her. She never tried to hurt anyone, never directly disobeyed the help, but instead tried to see just what she could get away with. If they ever did tell her to stop, or that it was finally bedtime, she would quietly comply.

Sometimes she seemed happy and fun-loving, enjoying wholeheartedly her wild outings and fantastic gifts. Yet this happiness was always fleeting, for Lisa knew that even after the divorce had been resolved, things still weren't right with her father. And try as she might, she didn't know how to make them better.

EIGHT

Please, Daddy, Don't Die!

★━━━━━━━━━━━━━━━━━━━━━━━━━━━━━━★

LISA AND ELVIS WERE BECOMING CLOSER THAN ever. By now it was clear she was going to be a beauty. Experienced beyond her years, she was a perfect companion for Elvis.

The days in California with her mother must have passed slowly without Elvis. Just school, homework, and chores around the house. Of course, there were always Priscilla's changing boyfriends. Now her mother was going out with another man. Mike Stone had been replaced by Priscilla's hairdresser, Elie Ezerzer.

In fact, Priscilla was trying to keep her romances secret from Lisa, at least for a while. Priscilla wanted her daughter's respect and would only have a boyfriend stay over after she knew it was going to be a serious relationship and had dated him for a while. Elvis was worried about how Priscilla's love life would affect Lisa. He told a confidant, "Priscilla's been a good mother, but I'll tell you this. I don't appreciate the fact that Lisa knows that other men sleep in the same bed with her unwed mother. It's not right. It can only confuse her head."

If home was not a particularly exciting environment, school also held little interest for Lisa. Although she was highly intelligent and perceptive, her natural inclination was toward understanding people, not books. After all, she'd already been exposed to so much that what she read in books must have seemed dry and dull in comparison. She was original, energetic, and clever, yet at times she must have seemed far-off to her teachers—a born daydreamer. And in some ways, they were right—her thoughts were elsewhere.

She would stare out the window. And when that expensive car pulled up to the school, she knew it was time. Elvis wanted her. He had called Priscilla from Las Vegas or wherever he

★

was touring and sent the *Lisa Marie* to pick his daughter up. Her exciting life, her real life, was about to begin.

As the jet took off, with its four full-time crew members tending to her every need, Lisa could look down on the dull world she left behind. Farewell to dirty dishes and vacuuming her room. She was going to see her daddy and become his little princess once again. As the jet engines whirled, the excitement in Lisa must have revved higher and higher. She was about to see her daddy . . . in concert.

Pittsburgh, 1976, New Year's Eve.

Eighteen inches of snow on the ground and still snowing hard. It was only five degrees above zero, but inside the Civic Center Arena you could feel the heat. Her grandfather Vernon escorted Lisa to her seat next to Ginger Alden, Elvis' current girlfriend.

She heard the chants from the crowd: "ELVIS! ELVIS! ELVIS!" In their private moments together, he was the man who would carry her on his shoulders and refer to her as Buttonhead. Now, he was something entirely different as he stood on the huge stage facing the 16,049 fans who had come to hear him this night. She saw this other side to him, the side the fans saw. No

longer "Elvis, my dad" but ELVIS PRESLEY—
the King.

While Lisa was sitting in her seat next to Ginger, Elvis was warming up behind stage, running through his karate motions, like a leopard
ready to pounce. His personal physician gave
him a shot of a quick pick-me-up right before
going on. Finally, to the regal theme from the
movie *2001* he appeared in the flesh, strutting
onto the stage with his white cape flowing after
him.

Lisa was temporarily blinded by the thousands of camera flashes. The fans were all taking pictures of her daddy, desperate for any
relics of their contact with him. Seeing him onstage was as close as most of them would ever
come.

And then Elvis began to sing. The voice
which sent chills up the spines of millions is-
sued forth.

It was a great show, even by Elvis' standards.
As he belted out "Reconsider Baby" he reached
everyone in the audience. He accompanied
himself on the piano on "Rags to Riches" and
"Unchained Melody" and the audience went
wild.

But certain songs, as always, seemed meant
for her alone. When Elvis sang "Separate Ways"
it was hard to imagine he could be thinking of

★

anything but his painful separation from Lisa and Priscilla.

Lisa saw her father the superstar onstage. The audience was completely under his spell. He was the great entertainer that everyone loved.

But there was another side to Elvis. He wasn't always like this. He needed love and support like everyone else. To the audience he was an invulnerable superstar, at the top of his form.

But in fact that night he was suffering from complaints that read like a medical dictionary: glaucoma, an enlarged heart, lupus erythematosus, persistent hypoglycemia, hypertension, a twisted colon, and arteriosclerosis.

And the drug problems were continuing. Uppers, downers, a confusing cornucopia of chemicals. Lisa had seen him popping pills: Demerol, Valium, Quaaludes, and others. She didn't really know what was going on but she couldn't have helped but notice the changes in Elvis' behavior —he was so erratic. Sometimes he seemed so incredibly energetic but other times he was sleeping so much, and even when he wasn't sleeping he seemed sluggish and his speech was slurred. Lisa, young as she was, knew that he wasn't well.

As Lisa flew back to California, her father's health must have weighed heavily upon her. Back in her dreary routine with Priscilla, her

★

life resumed its dull shape, yet her daddy was constantly on her mind.

In March, the expensive car pulled up again at school. She would be spending the weekend of the eighteenth with Elvis. This time Lisa was flown to Memphis, then whisked to Graceland itself.

Lisa was coming home. She hadn't been there since Christmas and the house bristled with excitement. The staff was busy completing their final preparations for Lisa's arrival. The cook was making Lisa's favorites: cornbread and black-eyed peas, and best of all, fried chicken, which had replaced hot dogs as the food she liked most. Lisa, like her father, loved traditional Southern cooking.

Lisa entered the house and felt the cold air. In the warmer months at Graceland the air-conditioning was constantly running, but even in March Elvis liked his home kept very cool. As was typical, he had the windows covered over so as to keep out any natural light, furthering the artificial and controlled effect Elvis preferred.

Elvis would typically wait for her in his bedroom. There, lying in his bed, he could see Lisa on the video monitors as she made her way through the house. He had had these installed when she was younger so he could keep an eye on her. Now that he was not as well, he used

★

them to see what was going on throughout the house when he was forced to stay in bed.

When Lisa saw her father, happy as she was, she had to have been stunned.

He looked so different. He had always had that faraway look in his eyes, but now he seemed increasingly removed from the world. He had gained some weight and was moving more slowly than he usually did. Still he was clearly happy to see her. He hugged her, calling her by his pet name for her—Buttonhead.

Later she would meet her father for breakfast in the Jungle Room, Elvis' favorite in the house. It overlooked the back lawns of Graceland. The room featured green shag carpeting on the ceiling as well as the floor. Elvis wanted a tropical effect and went all-out to get it.

Seven-feet-tall throne-like Polynesian Kon Tiki chairs were placed near mirrors framed by pheasant feathers. A special decorating touch was fake-fur lampshades. They hung over wooden bases carved with the faces of fierce Tiki deities. Elvis even saw to such details as rabbit-fur throw pillows and most importantly, a large working waterfall in the corner. It was in one of the large Hawaiian armchairs next to the waterfall that Lisa would often curl up and take her nap.

Elvis had miraculously decorated the entire room during a half-hour shopping spree at

★

Donald's of Memphis and had everything delivered that very day.

Graceland was still the same but Elvis' drug intake had increased. He was now at times irritable and cranky with the men who worked for him. So far he had never been this way with Lisa. With all the changes in both their lives, their relationship alone seemed secure.

But one time Lisa discovered that her golf cart—the toy which Elvis had given her and which provided them with hours of pleasure together—was broken. It had a flat tire.

Lisa ran to find her daddy. He would be able to fix it for her. She found him sitting on Graceland's patio, discussing his upcoming tour.

"Daddy, Daddy, my golf cart's broken. Will you come and fix it for me?"

"Buttonhead, I'm busy at the moment."

Lisa patiently waited for him to finish what he was doing. Then she expected that he would come and fix the flat tire.

But instead, Elvis continued to sit on the patio. When Lisa asked him again to help her, she still got no response. Lisa, however, was determined. Elvis looked up and snapped, "No, Lisa! Daddy doesn't do things like that."

But Lisa, every bit her father's daughter, showed her spunkiness and refused to take no for an answer. She teased him, taunting him

★

with "Maybe you don't know how to fix it. Maybe you can't do it."

Finally, Elvis put an end to the matter. "Lisa, baby, Daddy is rich. He doesn't have to do things like that. Yes, I know how to do it, but I pay people to do those things for me." He then dispatched a servant to tend to the repair. Lisa's daddy had changed so much.

What had happened to the father who had presented her with the poem "The Priceless Gift" and instructed her that money was not important? Before, he would have done anything for Lisa. Now, in a chemically sodden state, he seemed more detached.

Two weeks after this weekend visit with Lisa, Elvis was hospitalized. On April 1, 1977, he was admitted to Baptist Memorial allegedly for intestinal flu. But in fact, he was really there to dry out from the drugs he was taking.

During the stay he spoke freely to his nurse, Marian Cocke. Nurse Cocke states, "It was Lisa that was his favorite subject. How he loved that little girl. She really was the bright star in his life and he admitted he found it very hard to discipline her but that he tried to be a good daddy."

Priscilla and Lisa rushed to see him four days later on the day he was released. This was one of those rare and wonderful occasions when Lisa, Priscilla, and Elvis were together. How

★

special to be with both parents, even if only for a day.

Lisa looked into her father's eyes. The tacit bond contained in that look was reminiscent of the moment when Elvis first laid eyes on her, an infant cradled in Priscilla's arms in the very same hospital from which he had just been released. Then he would have done anything to protect Lisa. Now the roles were reversed. Elvis was the needy one and Lisa felt the need to take care of him. As she says today, "I was always protective of him."

Elvis was developing a dangerous obsession with guns. He had begun collecting simple handguns in 1969 after Sharon Tate's murder, fearful for Lisa's safety. But this natural desire to protect his family grew out of control, becoming not a mere hobby or a means to insure his family's safety, but a dangerous activity.

By the end of 1977, he would stroll into sporting goods stores and proceed to buy increasingly outrageous weapons. He purchased a nine-millimeter Beretta automatic with a pearl handle—James Bond's weapon—and a Walther PPK/S double-action automatic—the CIA's weapon. After seeing *Dirty Harry,* he knew he had to have the Colt .44 Magnum that Clint Eastwood favored, a gun that was capable of bringing down a small plane. In private, he wore the fully

★

loaded .44 Magnum in a massive shoulder holster, just like Clint did.

Other favorites were the 300 Magnum assassination rifle as well as an early .22 machine gun. Another prize was the Carl Hauptmann-Ferlach double-barreled rifle, the personal weapon of Hermann Göring. The Nazi had used it to slaughter thousands of wild beasts. An additional acquisition was a classic 1927 Thompson submachine gun, otherwise known as a tommy gun. And of course there were always the countless M-16's he kept around.

Collecting guns is one thing. Using them carelessly is another.

Once Elvis' girlfriend Linda Thompson was sitting in the bathroom of their penthouse suite at the Las Vegas Hilton. She heard a blast and simultaneously saw the toilet-paper roll on her right shred. A mirror in the room shattered. Pulling herself together, she quickly ran into the living room, frightened out of her wits.

Elvis was lounging on the living room sofa, his head resting on a pillow. He seemed completely serene as he held a still smoking .22 caliber Savage in his right hand.

Linda demanded to know what had happened.

Elvis was nonchalant. "Hey, hon, don't get excited."

Elvis was just doing some target-shooting in-

★

side the hotel suite and missed. The bullet had come within inches of killing Linda, but in his drugged state he didn't seem to react.

In any case, this crazed target-shooting would continue. Another night, it was the huge chandelier at the Imperial suite that dangled over his head. Taking careful aim he shot out every bulb until the chandelier itself came crashing down. The Hilton said nothing, although later the management put it on his bill.

Elvis also took to shooting out TV's whenever anything on them displeased him. He particularly disliked Robert Goulet and Mel Torme. Once in 1974 as Elvis was finishing breakfast, Goulet appeared on the set. Elvis casually put his knife and fork down, picked up a .22 and blasted him off the air and the TV to smithereens. He then picked up the knife and fork and began eating again.

As was usual, no one dared say anything. Elvis was the King, on stage and in his home, and no one questioned or criticized any of his actions, no matter how irrational. Only Lisa, asking with the innocence of a child but with the shrewdness of one who had witnessed much, could get through to Elvis. Everyone else was too afraid.

Innocently, but with genuine concern, seven-year-old Lisa, having seen the smashed TV, reproached her father.

★

"Daddy, why did you shoot the TV?"

Unable to look her in the eye, all that he could say to her was, "Aw honey, there was something on it that Daddy didn't like." He was like a guilty child, caught doing something he knew he shouldn't have.

Lisa had gotten through to him. True, Lisa could not prevent or completely stop his path of self-destruction. But she alone could reach Elvis in this period of outrageous excess.

"As his health declined in subsequent years, Lisa was the most important person in his life," Elvis' stepmother remembered in her memoir. "When his boredom and unhappiness reached rock-bottom, she cast the single beacon of brightness into the descending gloom. If there was one thing that compelled him forward when he was faltering, it was the continuing need to make his daughter proud of him."

Lisa was every inch daddy's little girl. If possible, the two grew even closer together.

Now when Lisa visited him on tour, Elvis was always sure to include Lisa in the spotlight too —something he rarely did for Priscilla when they were married. One night in Vegas, at the International, right after the thunderous ovation for "Hound Dog," he paused. Pointing to Lisa sitting in the booth in the front row, he introduced her, saying, "She takes over the whole house, she knows everybody's telephone numbers, she is just eight years old—my daughter, Lisa Marie."

The applause was just as thunderous as it had been for Elvis' singing. Lisa felt all eyes upon her but she took it like a true star, smiling in the spotlight. During that moment, father and daughter who had always been so close in private were now united in public.

Elvis may then have seemed to her immortal and all-powerful. But as soon as she sat back down again, her private concerns must have resurfaced. Despite the thrill of that moment, she always knew he was in trouble.

When she was only five, Lisa first mentioned the true nature of her concern to him. They were watching TV together. She turned to him and said, "Daddy, Daddy, I don't want you to die."

He looked down at her and said, "Okay. I won't. Don't worry about it."

He looked at her quizzically and then back at the TV set. But in some ways he understood.

As Lisa grew older these fears would not go away. Again and again she would repeat this same phrase to her father.

"Daddy, don't die. Please, Daddy, don't die."

NINE

My Daddy's Gone!

★————————————————————————————★

ELVIS HAD A DISTURBING DREAM. IN IT HE AND LISA
were together, making their way through post-
Apocalyptic Israel. As they traveled in a tank
through the mayhem and desolation around
them, Lisa began to weep. Elvis related his response to his spiritual adviser, Larry Geller. "I
look at her and I say 'Don't worry, don't worry.
Nothing's going to happen to your daddy—
there's always going to be an Elvis!'"

But by the summer of 1977, Elvis' health had

★

taken a turn for the worse. His weight had ballooned to 250 pounds from the 170 he weighed at the time of his comeback TV special. His heart was enlarged, colon twisted, and liver damaged. Elvis had trouble performing: he was forgetting lyrics and slurred those he could remember. Even when his performances were up to par, he would collapse afterward, slumped over in his dressing room.

His drug use had intensified. On one day alone Dr. Nichopolous (his personal physician) prescribed 100 tablets of Amytal and Quaaludes, 20 tablets of Biphetamine, and 50 tablets of Dilaudid in what, according to Dr. Nichopolous, was an attempt to control Elvis' use and wean Elvis from drugs. (Dr. "Nick" was later acquitted by a jury of criminal charges arising from his supplying such drugs to Elvis.) In fact, at this time, Elvis was averaging 25 pills or shots a day.

Elvis was able to ignore how he was deteriorating until the book *Elvis: What Happened?* was published. The book was written by Red and Sonny West and Dave Hebler (Elvis' bodyguards) and is now largely forgotten. But in July of 1977 it caused a sensation. Reported to be an exposé of Elvis, an inquiry into his decadent life-style and excesses, it left no slimy stone unturned, discussing everything from drug abuse to orgies.

★

Elvis was devastated. For years he had lived in a world without criticism. Like the emperor with no clothes, no one had dared to tell Elvis how self-destructive and decadent he had become. The book depicted Elvis' descent from a once sexy young rock star into a decayed, drugged, overweight, grotesquely distorted reflection of his former self.

Elvis was in agony about the drug disclosures. But why? It is not as self-evident as it seems.

His public loved him no matter what. The crowds in Vegas shrieked in ecstasy at the sight of him, however fat or medicated he was.

And Elvis' staff consisted of paid sycophants, men and women who worshiped Elvis without question. That was their job. They knew his excesses and this book contained nothing they were not already well aware of. The same held true for his girlfriends and buddies.

The painful disclosures of this book could hurt only one person—Lisa Marie.

Unlike the other people who passed through his world—girlfriends, bodyguards, backup singers, and servants—Lisa would always be a part of his life. Her image of him as a father was all-important. Elvis was anguished, literally heartsick, with the thought that Lisa would one day read the book and find out about his drug use. According to family intimates, this

★

fear was ultimately "crushing and desolating" for Elvis.

Desperate, Elvis once again considered death threats. According to Albert Goldman, Elvis asked his stepbrother David Stanley to hunt down Red and Sonny West, once his close friends and now authors of this cruel book. But David laughed him off, pointing out that Lisa "would be more ashamed of a father who was a murderer than one who was exposed as a drug addict." Elvis was brought to his senses.

Sickened, and disturbed by the book, Elvis had less than a month to live. He called for Lisa, for what would turn out to be her final visit. Priscilla readily sent her to see her father.

Lisa flew out on the *Lisa Marie* at the end of July in 1977. At Graceland, Elvis and Lisa played together as much as they could. Elvis, who now almost never went outdoors, would accompany Lisa as she drove her golf cart up and down Graceland's driveway.

On August 7, 1977, Elvis provided a special outing for Lisa. Lisa, Elvis, his current girlfriend Ginger and her niece Amber, and a few guests would be going to Liberty Land, an amusement park located in the Mid-South fairgrounds, ten miles from Graceland. Elvis had rented the entire park for the private party, closing it to the public for the night. The evening would begin at one in the morning and last

★

until dawn. Elvis loved bumper cars and roller coasters and in the 1950's rode them "wild style" —that is, without holding on.

Tonight was a different story. With Liberty Land's cheerful blue and white awnings and bright carnival lights as the backdrops, Elvis took no risks as he diligently went with Lisa from ride to ride.

The trip to Liberty Land, however, had almost been canceled by Elvis at the last minute for no reason at all. In his final months, he could be difficult, sometimes unaccountably irritable and erratic. Impulsively, on the night of the trip, he told Ginger they weren't going anymore. He was calling the evening off just because he felt like it, even though Ginger and Lisa had so looked forward to it.

"Why aren't we going?" Ginger demanded. "Everybody's dying to go. They're all ready."

Elvis thought up an excuse, saying everyone had already gone home.

Ginger challenged him, saying, "Elvis, I thought you once told me you could do anything."

Elvis, put to the test, realized the arbitrary and moody nature of his decision. He got on the phone and told Lisa, Amber, and the other guests that the trip was on again.

Later in the week, on Saturday the thirteenth of August, Elvis and Lisa had another outing—a

★

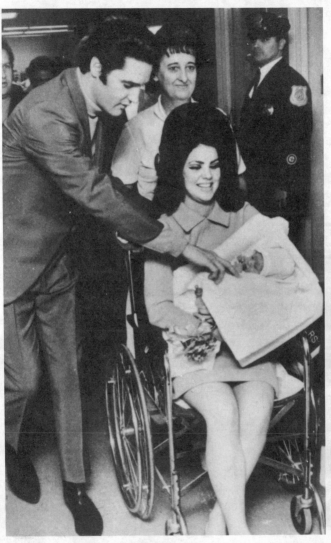

Elvis and Priscilla, leaving Baptist Memorial Hospital with newborn Lisa. *(Globe Photos)*

Left: Elvis as a child. Note Elvis's resemblance in this picture to nine-year-old Lisa *(below)*. *(Left: Globe Photos; Below: Frank Edwards/© Fotos International)*

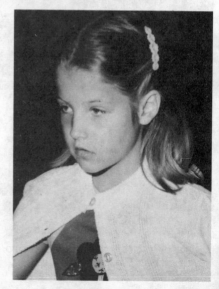

Elvis, in top form at a Vegas press conference, six months after Lisa was born. *(Frank Edwards/© Fotos International)*

Elvis's funeral procession in Memphis. Lisa sat in the first car. *(AP/Wide World Photos)*

Lisa during her awkward years gave only a hint of the beauty she would become. *(R.Dominguez/ Globe Photos)*

Priscilla, as always, fiercely guarding Lisa (then 13) from the press. Bloomingdale's, New York, 1981. *(© Ron Galella)*

The Apple School (now the Los Feliz Hills School), the
Scientology High School that Lisa attended as a troubled teen.
(Brian Bacchus)

Priscilla, Lisa, and Marco, in 1986. Priscilla is pregnant with
Navarone, her child by Marco. *(AP/Wide World Photos)*

Canter's–where it all began: a favorite hangout for Lisa, Danny, and D-BAT, the Scientology rock band that brought them together. *(Nicole Bettauer)*

Celebrity Centre International, the Scientology facility where Lisa lived and where her wedding was held. *(Brian Bacchus)*

Lisa and Danny on an early date, viewing a painting by Frank Frazetta at the L. Ron Hubbard Art Gallery in Los Angeles. Note L. Ron's portrait looming in the background. *(AP/Wide World Photos)*

Lisa with Danny, stepping out at the MTV Awards—finally taking her place in the spotlight. *(Steve Granitz/ © Celebrity Photo)*

Lisa, pregnant with Danielle, shops for groceries.
(© Rochelle Law/ Shooting Star)

Graceland from the Music Gate. Lisa returns several times a year to the home that is her inheritance.
(© Dagmar/Shooting Star)

typical night at the movies. Typical, that is, for Elvis Presley. He had rented an entire theater for a private late-night screening. Elvis would pay the projectionist to stay on until dawn. That Saturday, he and Lisa left Graceland at 3:30 A.M. in order to see *The Spy Who Loved Me.* Elvis loved James Bond movies and would bring his own gold-plated PK Walther gun. They only returned home at 6 A.M.

In the late afternoon on August 15, Elvis arose, had breakfast, and sent for Lisa. It was her last full day with him before her scheduled return to Beverly Hills. That night, after an invigorating day of playing with Lisa on Graceland's grounds, he requested an extra dose of sleeping medication. Lisa was returning to her mother the next day and he was about to begin his tour. Aunt Delta brought him sleeping pills.

Ginger and Elvis retired. He said to her, "Precious, I'm going to go into the bathroom and read for a while."

He carried with him *The Search for the Face of Jesus,* a book about the Holy Shroud of Turin. Lisa was fast asleep, as it was extremely late. The ensuing events of that fateful night are well known.

After Elvis entered the bathroom, Ginger fell sound asleep. She awoke around two in the afternoon and noticed Elvis had not returned to bed.

★

Ginger was not immediately concerned. She called her friend Cindy and chatted about the upcoming tour with Elvis. It was only then, when Elvis still had not returned to bed, that she got up and entered the bathroom.

It was there that she found Elvis, collapsed on the floor with the book by his side. Even after she saw him, Ginger was not unduly alarmed. He often fell asleep in odd places or positions because of the pills he took. The medication could suddenly take effect and knock him out at any moment.

But when she turned him over and felt how rigid he was, Ginger began to panic. Then she saw the discolored face and the protruding tongue and screamed for help. It was the subsequent hysteria that attracted Lisa's attention.

Soon the paramedics arrived and removed Elvis from the house. Lisa was still hysterical from the brief glimpse she saw in the bathroom. Ginger sought out the little girl, who was whimpering in her room. She tried to comfort her and calm her down.

Ginger tried to reason with Lisa. Ginger, along with everyone else in the house, was not completely certain that Elvis was really dead. After all, they still had not heard from the hospital. Perhaps he was merely suffering from a mild overdose.

"Lisa, your daddy's going to be okay."

★

Lisa had to believe her. Soon she was frolicking with her friend Amber and thinking nothing was wrong.

Meanwhile, the ambulance sped up Route 51 —now renamed Elvis Presley Boulevard—to Baptist Memorial, the hospital where Lisa was born.

Extensive measures were taken in a desperate attempt to revive Elvis. Inside trauma room number one, doctors wired electrodes in an attempt to electrically start his heart beating again. They strapped wires to his bloated chest. Electricity surged through his inert body. Still, he did not move.

They then tried mechanical respiration, forcing air in and out of his lungs, imitating the natural act of breathing.

Next, he was injected with long needles containing strong stimulants in yet another feverish attempt to bring him round.

Finally, after half an hour of repeated and intensive efforts, his physicians gave up. His case was declared hopeless.

Elvis Presley was dead.

On some level the doctors probably knew that they could have done nothing. All of their efforts were hopeless. From the first they must have known they were striving in vain. In fact, the doctors eventually classified the patient as DOA, dead on arrival.

★

While the official cause of the death was "cardiac arrhythmia" or an erratic heartbeat, doctors found a mixture of chemicals in his bloodstream—one that is difficult to believe yet was typical for Elvis in the last years of his life.

These included codeine (at ten times the dosage that might have killed a person unused to it), morphine, Quaaludes (also at a deadly level), Demerol, and Valium.

Dr. Nick now had the difficult task of telling the family that Elvis was dead. He returned to Graceland. Instantly, at the mere sight of him, everyone knew. Dr. Nick could only say, "I'm sorry."

Lisa, who had been lulled into a false sense of security, now had to face the truth. Lisa screamed and screamed. "I can't believe my daddy is gone!" She rushed to call her mother.

"Mommy, Mommy. Something's happened to Daddy."

"I know, baby," Priscilla replied. (She had been told moments before by Joe Esposito.) "I'll be there soon. I'm waiting for the plane now."

"Everybody's crying, Mommy."

Priscilla could do nothing more for Lisa and immediately headed to the airport, where the *Lisa Marie* had been sent for her.

At Graceland, there were other calls to be made.

★

Lisa herself dialed Linda Thompson, one of Elvis' old girlfriends.

"He's gone," she blurted out through tears to the former Miss Tennessee.

"No, Lisa, I'm sure he's just resting," Linda insisted.

"No, Linda, he's dead. My daddy's dead."

Linda too would return to Graceland.

Soon, Lisa went outside and got out her golf cart. Lisa drove around and around Graceland, confused and bewildered by events which, as a nine-year-old, she could not fully understand.

When Priscilla arrived at two-thirty in the morning, she found Lisa still circling on her golf cart.

"Is it true?" Lisa asked. "Is my daddy really gone?"

Priscilla nodded. She embraced her daughter. Lisa walked back to her golf cart and resumed riding.

She drove by herself in the hot Tennessee night. Lisa, fundamentally alone in her grief, played with the favorite toy her father had given her. No words could fully comfort her or ease her pain. Eerily she circled the house where she'd grown up, driving on and on through the night, alone on her golf cart, her father never again to be by her side.

TEN

THE FUNERAL

★————————————————————————★

LISA'S LOSS, GREAT AS IT WAS, WAS SHARED BY MIL-
lions. Within an hour of the announcement of
Elvis' death, as Lisa struggled in disbelief and
shock behind the gates of Graceland, thousands
of fans began to line up outside. By the next day,
eighty thousand mourners were waiting in a
line which stretched for a mile along Elvis Presley Boulevard.

They'd come from everywhere. Not just Memphis and the rest of Tennessee, but from all over

the country. They felt compelled to be there to see Elvis one last time. Many just took off and headed for Graceland, leaving jobs and loved ones behind. A young housewife from the Midwest abandoned her children, ages two, four, and five, to the care of a twelve-year-old babysitter, in order to pay her final respects to the King.

As the crowd first assembled outside Graceland's gate, they were silent. People were lost in their grief, often sinking to their knees and sobbing into their hands. But by the second day, the mood had changed to one of latent outrage and anger that the King was dead.

There were scuffles in the ever-increasing lines. Helicopters flew overhead, scanning the mobs for possible signs of violence. Eventually the National Guard was called in and a sentry was placed in front of the house to guard Lisa and the rest of the family.

To the throngs outside the gates, Elvis belonged to them. They grieved for their own loss, the loss of the King. To them he was not a father or a husband . . . he was just Elvis. Few considered how great the loss must have been for those truly most affected, his daughter and family. They thought of themselves first, not of Lisa.

One Memphis matron, Judy Rae, had an unusual initial reaction. She was in Baptist Memorial Hospital visiting her sick mother at the time Elvis was admitted.

She remembers seeing a large motorcade outside the emergency room. The nurses joked that it must be Elvis—who else could own so many cars! Then the news came through that it actually was Elvis and that he had died. Judy Rae was shocked and grief-stricken. The nurses began crying. A feeling of gloom descended upon the wards throughout the hospital. Judy Rae could not believe it. The legendary Elvis was dead. But Judy Rae, a mother of three, unlike most of the fans, then thought of Elvis' child. She said to her mother, "Poor little Lisa. Poor little Lisa. She's lost her daddy. She'll have all his millions but what will she do without Elvis? Poor thing!" Judy was one of the few of Elvis' mourners who considered Lisa's loss alongside her own.

At Graceland, the crowds continued to surge. A cry arose when they caught sight of the motorcade bearing Elvis' body back to Graceland in preparation for the funeral. It was to be held on the next day, the eighteenth of August at two o'clock in the afternoon. The music gates were opened to allow the gruesome procession to pass through. These gates were guarded by twelve policemen who quickly shut them after the hearse entered, in order to repel the overwrought, grief-stricken crowd.

Inside the house, the massive coffin was wheeled in and placed in Graceland's formal entrance hall, the same hall where only nine years before the vital, healthy Elvis had carried his newborn daughter. With the National Guardsmen guarding the front door, the nine-hundred-pound, copper-lined coffin was set beneath the crystal chandelier.

Vernon, mourning the loss of his son, consented to a two-hour public viewing. At three o'clock, the fans were to be allowed into Graceland. Lisa was ushered out and kept away from the crowd.

When the gates were swung open, the lines to get in extended for miles. As it was already 90 degrees, many people collapsed from the sweltering heat. The Red Cross established first-aid centers in tents on the lawns of Graceland to attend to the injured faithful.

Only the lucky ones got inside the house—just a small fraction of the crowd of eighty thousand fans could possibly be accommodated. For years the fans had been kept outside the music gates. Only now, under such tragic circumstances, could they enter.

Elvis was laid out in a blue shirt, a light gold tie, and a white suit that Vernon had given him for Christmas. On his finger was the diamond and gold ring emblazoned with his trademark TCB—"Taking Care of Business."

★

As the mourners filed past Elvis' coffin, their hearts were heavy. They were filled with grief but at least they had the chance to see Elvis one last time. But what of the other fans, those who were kept outside in the blistering heat?

Vernon realized that he had to extend the hours for the viewing by an hour and a half, until 6:30 P.M. But even then, only a small additional fraction of the fans could be admitted.

When it was announced that no more fans would be allowed in, there was a tremendous outcry from the mob. Screams of "No! No!" punctuated the summer heat. Would the crowds rush the house? The National Guard was ready, with troops in formation behind the gate and reinforcements on call.

But no riot ensued. The mournful crowd, still in a state of shock, simply dispersed. People were alone again in their sorrow.

Later, Lisa and Priscilla gathered before the casket for a private moment alone to say their good-byes. After the last fans from the public viewing had filtered out, Lisa and her mother stood before the coffin, which had been moved to the music room in preparation for the funeral. No other members of the family were present. Lisa stepped slowly up to the coffin.

The sight she saw must have truly upset Elvis' daughter. The beloved father she had played with just days before was now a disfig-

★

ured corpse. Elvis' face was still swollen; the blood had settled in his head and expanded his once handsome features. The blood cast a purplish tint to his skin that makeup could not hide, particularly the discolorations underneath the eyes. It was strange to see the father who had been so full of life only days before now so incredibly still.

As Priscilla recounts the moment in *Elvis and Me,* she said to her former husband's corpse:

"You look so peaceful, Satnin. I know you'll find happiness and all the answers there . . . Just don't cause any trouble at the pearly gates."

Lisa then touched her father for the very last time. She placed on his right wrist a silver bracelet portraying the joined hands of a mother and child. Together they said their last private good-bye. "We'll miss you."

Around four A.M., a crowd was still assembled outside Graceland's stone walls when, suddenly, disaster struck. A white Ford truck ran into the mourners. Two fans—Juanita Joanne Johnson and Alice Marie Hovartar, who had traveled from Monroe, Louisiana—were killed instantly and many more were injured.

When the crowd saw what had happened, they tried to charge the car, which had stopped a block away. "Lynch him! String him up!" the angry mob shouted at the driver. Their emotions were extremely volatile, strained and ago-

★

nized by their grief for Elvis. The police intervened, rescuing the driver from the crowd's wrath.

The accident outside only added to the horror and unreality inside the house.

The family members were now gathered in the den. Although some were still crying, Lisa had finally begun to calm down.

She was only nine years old, with a limited understanding of death. Yet so much still weighed on her mind. Tomorrow was the funeral. She knew that it was *her* daddy, and hers alone, that was gone. But there were thousands of people lined up outside the gates to her home who mourned him in a different way: not as a father but as a superstar.

She tried to reconcile the two images, combining what she was hearing from her family with what she was hearing on the news.

When Lisa entered the room where the family members were gathered, she said without passion, as if she were just another fan, "You know, I just can't believe it: Elvis Presley is dead."

Perhaps nine-year-old Lisa understood more at the formal funeral services the next day. The services were held at 2:00 P.M. in the music room. Lisa sat in the front row, flanked by her mother and grandfather. Behind her sat the rest of the family, and celebrities such as Ann-Margret, George Hamilton, and Chet Atkins. Seven

★

speakers, including the comedian Jackie Kahane, gave eulogies that spoke of Elvis' warmth and generosity.

As the service was ending, Lisa's grandfather suddenly rose from her side and shouted at the coffin, "Son, I'll be with ya soon! Son, I'll be with ya soon!"

Dodger was beside herself with grief and also burst into tears.

Lisa sat next to her relatives, bewildered and frightened as they disintegrated into unmitigated grief and hysteria. Tears overflowed as she wept for her daddy.

There were reminders of him everywhere, reminders of how much he meant to so many people.

Over three thousand bouquets had been flown in from around the world. Every flower in Memphis flower shops had been sent to Graceland. It was almost impossible to find a blossom anywhere in Memphis other than at the Presley estate.

All the flags in the states of Mississippi and Tennessee were lowered to half-mast. President Carter offered his condolences, saying, "Elvis' death deprives our country of a part of itself."

It had become a day of national mourning, almost like the Kennedy funeral, when the entire country grieved as one. Like little John-John Kennedy, Lisa Marie stoically faced the un-

★

timely death of a young father. Yet unlike at Kennedy's death, where national attention was focused on his children and widow, Lisa was largely ignored by the national media. Though her pain was no doubt as great as that suffered by the Kennedy children at their father's loss, it was not the subject of national concern. Instead all attention was focused on Elvis.

Interestingly, Caroline Kennedy was at the funeral, covering it for *Rolling Stone* magazine. However, rather than extending sympathy to the family, some felt she treated them with condescension.

Caroline seemed to poke fun at the decor of the house and the friendly, informal manner with which people behaved. For example, she dwelled upon Graceland's furnishings: "a clear-glass statue of a nude woman stood high off the floor, twirling slowly, adorned by glass beads that looked like water," "plastic palms surrounded the coffin and on the wall was a painting of a skyline on black velveteen."

She mentioned Lisa only in passing, noting that she was somewhere in the house when Elvis died. Their backgrounds could not have been more different, but Caroline and Lisa had both lost famous fathers when young. Nonetheless, Caroline chose not to empathize with Lisa.

After the funeral, Lisa, Priscilla, and Vernon

★

drove to the cemetery. The three-mile route was lined by thousands of mourning fans.

The funeral procession was eighteen cars long. The first car was an enormous silver limousine, which was followed by the hearse and then by sixteen white Cadillacs carrying the rest of the mourners. Helicopters trailed overhead.

They traveled in the blistering heat, like a royal procession. Soon they would lay the body in a marble crypt and bow their heads in prayer.

Lisa sat in that enormous limousine, with her mother and her grandfather. The nine-year-old was watched by the helicopters and the curious crowds. The car continued on its relentless path toward her daddy's burial.

She now had everything and nothing. Elvis, her daddy, was dead. And though she couldn't have realized what it all meant, his fortune and his legacy now belonged not to the fans, not to Priscilla, nor to Elvis' girlfriends or managers, but to her—Lisa Marie Presley.

ELEVEN

THE WILL

★————————————————————★

ELVIS' WILL, ALTHOUGH THIRTEEN PAGES LONG, was very simple. Lisa Marie was his sole heir. Vernon was the executor. Vernon and Grandma Minnie Mae could share in the estate and would be provided for until their deaths, at which point the estate would all become Lisa's. No mention was made of Priscilla or Ginger or any other girlfriend or companion. According to a stipulation of the will, Lisa would receive everything when she turned twenty-five.

★

Elvis left much behind him. At the National Bank of Commerce his checking account had a balance of $1,055,173. He also had numerous savings accounts, some with small balances and others with up to $35,000 in them.

Lisa would also inherit all of Elvis' spectacular possessions. In addition to the *Lisa Marie* (the Convair 880 jet), he left another plane—a nine-passenger Jet Star. There were also eight cars and jeeps including a 1971 Stutz Blackhawk, seven motorcycles, and several golf carts.

Elvis had twenty pairs of pajamas, 242 chairs and couches, and several statues—including the one Caroline Kennedy noticed. The entire inventory of his holdings was seventy-six pages long.

And finally, not only would Lisa inherit all this, but also Graceland itself, her childhood home.

Although by all appearances enormously rich, in two years' time it would become clear that the estate was in a much shakier financial position than anyone could have imagined. But for the moment, it was believed to be the richest estate on record in Tennessee.

At the family dinner after the funeral—mostly cold platters brought in by a caterer—Lisa was just a normal nine-year-old eating a sandwich and trying to sort out the day's events.

★

Little did she know that she was in effect the richest person at the table and they were eating in the house that she would soon own. Priscilla, however, was quite aware of this.

But no matter how rich she was, what little Lisa needed most was understanding and comfort. She turned to the staff of Graceland as well as her family, people that she had grown up with and that had worshiped her father. Dick Grobe was the head of security and hence was very protective of Lisa. Lisa had heard that Dick had suffered a similar loss as a child—his father had died when he was very young.

In the days after the funeral, she sought out Dick. He comforted her as they drove in the golf cart around the grounds of Graceland.

"You'll get over the loss. The world isn't going to stop. But you'll always have the memories." Dick reports that Lisa "accepted that."

Yet Lisa's suffering was far from over. Such a difficult and sudden loss would take time for her to recover from. As a rich nine-year-old without her protective father, Lisa's problems had only begun.

Now, there was a family conference over what to do next with her. Vernon was in favor of keeping her at Graceland, close to the memory of her father and the rest of the Presley family. Her mother, however, wanted to take her back to Beverly Hills. Priscilla prevailed.

★

Back in Beverly Hills, Priscilla sent Lisa away to summer camp while she planned their next move. At summer camp, Lisa would be away from the prying press and the relentless gossip. There, with Debbie and Cindy, the children of Joe and Joannie Esposito—Joe was Elvis' best man and Joannie was a good friend of Priscilla's—she might find some peace. Debbie and Cindy had known Lisa for years and would no doubt be a familiar and consoling presence in this difficult time.

After this brief retreat, Priscilla put her plans into effect. Along with Priscilla's sister Michelle, Lisa and her mother set off secretly for a long trip to Europe.

This trip might distract the troubled child and raise her spirits. According to friends, despite all the interesting sights and tourist attractions of Europe, Lisa's mood was not lifted. The child was continually somber. Lisa, once so outgoing and sunny, could barely manage a smile at the colorful European scenes she witnessed. Where had the child in Lisa gone?

And there were the nightmares, horrible and frightening, according to a confidante. Elvis' death had to have haunted her dreams, supplying vivid and gruesome images. She would wake up crying and seek out her surviving parent for consolation. Priscilla was there to comfort her, but Priscilla had fears of her own.

★

It was widely and incorrectly rumored that Lisa had inherited $150 million dollars. Given her famous name and place in the spotlight, Lisa was a prime target for a kidnapping attempt. Among the legions of Elvis' fans looking for mementos of the King, it is also possible that there were a few disturbed individuals who might snatch Lisa for her name alone. Priscilla thought Lisa might be safer in Europe from both kidnappers and the press. She decided to enroll Lisa in a European boarding school.

But this was not to be. Reportedly, Lisa was rejected by school after school in England, Switzerland, and Italy. Priscilla had selected for Lisa schools attended by the children of European royalty and rich Arab students. Yet accustomed as these schools were to the children of kings, Lisa, the daughter of the King, was simply too great a security risk. Where could they go? Was there anywhere they could find peace and get on with their lives now that Elvis was gone?

Mother and daughter returned home to Beverly Hills, prepared to transform their home into a veritable fortress. According to published accounts, they took drastic measures to insure Lisa's safety. Electronic alarm systems were placed along the gates and house. Vicious guard dogs patrolled the grounds, trained to kill. TV cameras monitored anyone approaching the

★

gate and flashed the image into the house for a careful security check. It got to the point where Priscilla reportedly would not even admit close family members without scanning them on the TV camera and sending out a guard to search behind them for hidden intruders.

But whatever security precautions Priscilla may have taken, she still sought to give Lisa as normal a childhood as possible, given the circumstances. Priscilla didn't want to let Lisa's fame and fortune and their accompanying dangers overwhelm the way she raised her daughter. Although she was cautious, the two tried not to become hermits, living in isolation, withdrawn from the world.

As Lisa remembers, despite their precautions, she was not raised as "a little bodyguarded celebrity child." Even now she says that in public "I don't disguise myself with floppy hats or sunglasses, [though] I don't want people following me around."

However well mother and daughter were coping with their loss, it was not going to be easy setting up a new life. The outside world was not all they had to fear. Despite the elaborate security measures, the high walls, the wires, the guards, and the cameras, there were problems within the house. Tensions were growing in their protected world, tensions that no security measures could eliminate.

★

TWELVE

THE EMPIRE CRUMBLES

★────────────────────────────────────★

IF LISA COULD NOT BE ENROLLED IN A EUROPEAN school, Priscilla found the next-best thing—a European-style school in America, the Los Angeles Lycée Français. Lisa began attending the exclusive Lycée, located in Culver City, in the fall of 1977.

The Lycée, with its curriculum stressing French language and literature, is famed for its erudite and secluded atmosphere. It was perfect

★

for someone trying to stay out of the public's eye.

Such stars as Jodie Foster, and the children of famous Hollywood directors like Adrian Lynne *(Fatal Attraction)* attended the Lycée. Along with young Hollywood royalty, the school also boasted the children of numerous wealthy Europeans.

Lisa was enrolled in the American section of the school, where the classes, except for French, were taught in English. Priscilla had wanted her to be bilingual, but it proved much too difficult for this all-American girl from Memphis.

But at least this new atmosphere could assist in putting the painful memories she had behind her. The academic demands and the day-to-day routine would help make Lisa focus on the present.

But that aching loss must have always been there, even if she wasn't aware of it. Although Lisa was not obsessed with the tragedy in an unhealthy way, at home there were subtle reminders of the good times.

While the presence of Elvis was not overwhelming, there were pictures of him throughout the house. In the main hall, Elvis' famous Gold Sunglasses, the ones that had his initials "EP" on the nosebridge, were prominently displayed on a pedestal. But Lisa's room, the room farthest away in the most remote part of the

★

house, showed her devotion to him. There an entire wall was covered with images of Elvis encased in clear plastic frames with red edges.

Lisa was still mourning Elvis, and her grief was taking the natural healing process step by step. The sudden shock was over. Lisa was coping more and more, each day moving forward with her own young life.

This step-by-step healing process was aided by a home life finally stable after so many upheavals. She had already been through so much at such a young age, and now at last things were beginning to settle down. But this newfound stability which Lisa so desperately needed was interrupted when her mother took a new lover, Michael Edwards.

Edwards was a supermodel, earning large amounts of money and leading a glamorous life as one of the handsomest men in the world. He was at the top of his career and was sought after in Europe, New York, and Los Angeles when he met Priscilla at a party at her home in Beverly Hills. He immediately hit it off with Lisa's mother and was soon to become a permanent part of both of their lives.

While Lisa was still ten, Michael Edwards tried to get to know the daughter of his lover and the King. At first Lisa was very distant. He tried to break the ice by asking her questions. In some ways these questions were harmless con-

★

versation but they were also pointed, sometimes even intimate, coming from a near stranger.

Once when they were alone in the kitchen, he asked her, "You ever think about singing?"

"Not really. I don't think Mommy would let me," Lisa replied.

"I know you have a pretty voice. I've heard you in your room."

Elvis' daughter quickly moved the topic away from her voice.

"I took piano lessons once."

"Did you like it? Why don't you continue . . . ? It would have pleased your dad, I bet."

Lisa would have no more of this conversation.

"Cut this [mango] up for me like you do," Lisa demanded.

Tough little Lisa refused to answer any more of his questions. Who was this man telling her what her father would or would not have liked?

"If you say please," Edwards continued.

"Please."

Lisa's flat answers indicated she must have found it intrusive so soon after her own loss to have a stranger examining her in this way. But what must have made it more painful was that this overly curious stranger had seduced her mother.

Priscilla was soon totally caught up in her whirlwind romance with Edwards—dancing all

★

night, coming home at dawn, and making love not only in the bedroom, but also in the kitchen and even the servants' quarters.

Edwards moved into the house. Before, Lisa could avoid this star-struck intruder when he arrived to pick her mother up for another evening on the town. Now, he was there all the time: when Lisa woke up in the morning, when he picked her up from school.

Edwards asserted himself in his new role as man of the house—in some ways he gradually tried to usurp the role of her recently dead father. He tried to change Lisa, to make her into something she wasn't.

Like her father, Lisa had simple, down-home tastes. Although Elvis made hundreds of millions of dollars, he stayed loyal to the family, friends, and values he had grown up with. A good time for him meant amusement parks, go-carts, and lots of hamburgers.

Edwards, although originally from Pensacola, Florida, had fancier, European-influenced aspirations. He imposed these tastes on Lisa.

For example, Edwards sought to teach her about continental cuisine. He insisted Lisa accompany him on dates with Priscilla to expensive restaurants in order to "refine" her tastes and make her partake in the family he was trying to create.

But Lisa was not won over.

★

"I don't like to sit in some dumb restaurant for hours listening to you guys talking all the time. It's boring, boring, boring."

Like most ten-year-olds, Lisa preferred a hamburger at McDonald's to a fancy restaurant. Elvis would have, too. But Edwards was determined.

"I think you should learn about good restaurants for when you begin dating, Lisa."

"Whoever I date is going to take me to McDonald's or I'm not going out with him," Lisa retorted.

Lisa was not going to give up who she was without fighting.

The battle of wills intensified. As the weeks went by, Lisa's desires were increasingly placed second to Edwards'.

"Mommy, can't you guys do something besides going out to dinner all the time?"

"What would you like to do, Lisa?"

"Go to Magic Mountain or something fun."

Edwards proposed a barbecue instead.

"That's still eating," Lisa countered.

They left for the barbecue, which was to be held at the beach. As usual Edwards had prevailed. Even though her father also wanted to raise Lisa properly, at least he would have taken into account what she wanted.

Once they finally got to the beach, sand got into their food and it began to rain. Edwards' plan was a disaster. Edwards admitted that Lisa was right—Magic Mountain Amusement Park would probably have been a better idea.

"Huh, it's a little late," was all Lisa could say.

Just two years before, Lisa had spent happy hours at Liberty Land with her father, when the King rented out the entire park for Lisa and his guests. There, they played together on the bumper cars. Now, with her father gone, the new man in the household did not seek to share these innocent pleasures.

Glumly and stoically, Lisa faced the new situation.

Finally her problems with Edwards came to a head over a side issue: the housekeepers (a live-in married couple) were quitting. They had been a continuing, stable presence in Lisa's life since the move to California. Their leaving only aggravated Lisa's already inflamed sense of instability and loss. She blamed Edwards for their departure.

"If you didn't drink so much around them, they'd still be here."

Edwards denied that his drinking had anything to do with it.

Priscilla took Edwards' side, saying that the couple had other reasons for leaving.

Lisa was not convinced. "They left because of Michael."

But did it really matter why they had left?

★

The fact was, Lisa was losing more people she loved. She asked helplessly, "What am I supposed to do now? Who have I got to talk to?"

Enrolled in a school where they didn't even speak English, her mother's attention diverted by a new man, and living away from Graceland and her roots—Lisa was emotionally isolated. The impact of her father's loss was never more painfully clear.

Edwards admits that he and Priscilla were placing Lisa after their romance and careers. "We were so caught up with each other that we were neglecting Lisa," he confesses in his memoir *Priscilla, Elvis, and Me.* Increasingly, they dumped Lisa with Priscilla's parents whenever they wanted to be alone.

Real-life drama merged with celluloid fantasy when Edwards landed a role in the movie *Mommie Dearest* starring Faye Dunaway as Joan Crawford. In his only scene, he plays Joan Crawford's lover, whose presence tears Joan and her daughter Christina apart.

The scene opens as he and Joan begin to make passionate love. Christina walks in on them. He sees the little girl in the doorway and utters his big line: "We've got company." Joan, enraged by the intrusion, banishes Christina to boarding school.

Ironic real-life parallels to this movie scene abound. Edwards was indeed the lover of a fa-

★

mous actress. And this actress had a young daughter who was also sometimes inadvertently in the way. Although Priscilla was no Joan Crawford, Edwards tells many stories of Lisa being sent away, leaving them alone with each other.

Lisa herself, disturbed by the changes in her environment, was saying, "I want to go back to Memphis. I don't like it here anymore."

Lisa could find peace at Graceland, even if L.A. was not a happy place. She returned frequently. Though Elvis was dead, Graceland was maintained as he left it—as a private home.

Mary Jenkins was still cooking up Lisa's favorite fried chicken in the kitchen. Vernon and Grandma Minnie Mae were there to welcome her. Elvis' double first cousin Patsy lived nearby, as did Lisa's childhood friends. Even Elvis' dog was still there, now cared for by Aunt Delta who lived downstairs.

There, surrounded by loving relatives and familiar servants, the warm feelings at Graceland were almost as they used to be before.

Lisa slept downstairs now. Since Elvis died, she no longer occupied her old upstairs bedroom down the hall from his suite—the place where she found his body.

The difficulties of her life in California were literally worlds away. So much of what she had loved had been taken away from her. But if ev-

★

erything else in her life was subject to upheaval, at least Graceland would always be there for her.

Or so everyone thought.

Priscilla was stunned to learn about the dismal financial condition of the estate. After Vernon's quiet death in 1979, Priscilla with Joseph Hanks (Elvis' longtime accountant) and the National Bank of Commerce were named co-executors. Hanks brought Priscilla up to date, telling her the grim truth.

By the end of 1979, it cost the estate $480,000 a year to keep Graceland maintained. Most of the cost was for security, taxes, and insurance. However, the estate was barely bringing in enough to meet these costs. Within ten years, with Elvis gone and no new records or movies coming out, it was expected that the estate would not be able to meet its expenses. By the time Lisa inherited her trust at twenty-five, there would be nothing left for her.

In fact, the threat of bankruptcy approached much more swiftly. In 1981, the IRS reappraised the estate, taking into account all the royalties it had received since Elvis' death. The news was bleak—the estate would have to pay a $10 million inheritance tax, more money than it had on hand. There didn't seem to be a way out.

Lisa might suddenly have nothing but a famous name. All that Elvis had worked for in

★

order to make her life easier than his might be lost. When he was alive, he had tried to give her everything but now that he was dead, Lisa could end up with nothing.

How could it have come to this, four short years after her father's death? Where had all the money gone? Elvis had made $100 million during his lifetime but now his daughter was nearly penniless.

The answer lay not with Elvis or Priscilla but with Elvis' business manager, Colonel Tom Parker.

The Colonel's alleged misdealings were uncovered when Priscilla and her co-executors filed routine papers with the court. Judge Evans, apparently troubled by the unusually large commissions the Colonel was extracting from the estate, appointed a Memphis attorney—Blanchard E. Tual—to investigate. Tual became guardian *ad litem* for Lisa Marie—that is, temporary guardian for her financial affairs concerning the estate.

Tual uncovered what he considered to be misdealings by the Colonel. Priscilla and the co-executors had been prepared to continue their arrangements with Parker indefinitely. Without Tual, there is no telling what further damage might have been done.

Tual uncovered great irregularities in the Colonel's deals. The Colonel sold all future rights

★

and royalties of Elvis' recordings made before 1973 to RCA Records for $5.4 million. After taxes, Elvis received only half of this, only $1.35 million dollars. Although this might seem like a lot, the meager nature of this deal becomes clear when compared to the royalty earnings of other rock stars. For example, it has been estimated that John Lennon made over $300 million primarily from royalties.

Tual filed a report in court to Judge Evans chronicling in detail what he found to be Parker's extensive mismanagement. Judge Evans ordered that the estate sever dealings with Parker and a lawsuit against him began. It was settled with a payment to Parker for two million dollars to effectively end Parker's lifelong involvement with Elvis' profits. The executors regained all merchandising and licensing rights.

Still, even with the Colonel gone and financial affairs more in order, the estate faced the problem of bankruptcy. There seemed to be no way to pay the inheritance taxes it owed the IRS. There was no way to come up with ten million dollars. The unimaginable was about to occur. If the estate went bankrupt, Graceland would have to be sold.

THIRTEEN

THE DARK CLOUD

★——————————————————————★

BACK IN LOS ANGELES, UNAWARE OF WHAT WAS happening to her fortune, Lisa was withdrawn from the Lycée by her mother. The students were too Hollywood for Priscilla. And the school was too difficult academically. As Priscilla admits, neither she nor Lisa were stellar students —"We're both more for the fun."

She chose a much more secluded environment for Lisa: the Apple School, a school

★

founded by a group of Scientologists which featured Scientology teachings.

Priscilla had been actively involved with Scientology for several years. According to Edwards, John Travolta introduced her to the movement over lunch, stressing its positive benefits. Although the Apple School was not directly affiliated with the church, it used Scientology-based teaching.

All the regular subjects were taught, but individuals progressed at their own rate, studying on their own schedule. Thus, in the same classroom, one student might be studying advanced math and another beginning French.

Central to the study technique, derived from L. Ron Hubbard's teaching, was the concept that all abstractions had to be modeled out with real objects for complete comprehension. In Scientology jargon, this technique balanced the significance of the written word with physical mass, avoiding the problem of misunderstood words—a key issue for Scientologists.

To this end, each student was given a demo kit which contained clay and other real-life objects for modeling, in order for them to understand abstract concepts.

For example, in French class, students might be taught the phrase *"Je t'aime"*— I love you. To prove they understood, they would use the Scientology Study Tech, taking out their demo

★

kit and demonstrating this idea with objects. They would take two sticks or create two clay figures and make them "kiss" each other, proving they knew exactly what the foreign phrase *"Je t'aime"* meant. This individually paced method was perhaps better suited to Lisa after the more traditional rigors of the French Lycée.

The Apple School is located in the Los Feliz Hills section of Los Angeles near the famous Hollywood sign.

The close-knit community of students must have wondered what Lisa would be like. There was no hubbub when she arrived, but people were keenly aware that the King's daughter was in their midst.

Lisa was not the spoiled and arrogant celebrity child they had expected. Instead, they found that she was a deeply troubled, even morose girl who wasn't outgoing and often kept to herself. Rather than calling attention to herself, she seemed to fade into the woodwork. In her classes she would hang back, rather than fully participating. Teachers would try to get her involved, but it was a difficult task, requiring a great deal of energy for the most minimal response.

So reluctant was she to participate or get involved that she would sometimes duck out of a class altogether. Lisa would simply disappear

★

just like she had at Graceland when Mary's back was turned.

The teachers knew that something was wrong. Said one, "Lisa needed something. You could tell something wasn't right."

Her performance teacher was particularly concerned. In this class as in her others, Lisa held back. The teacher spotted innate but undeveloped talent, not necessarily that of singer but visible in Lisa's sense of rhythm and artistic expression and understanding.

Lisa, however, didn't believe in herself. She wouldn't try hard enough to make these talents come to fruition.

The teacher took her aside, trying to reach her. She told Lisa that she had real potential, but she needed to start working if she was going to develop it.

Lisa listened to everything but said nothing. She nodded her head in silent agreement as if she understood. But she never opened up about what was really troubling her.

Sometimes Lisa's withdrawal became belligerent. Her steadfast refusal to participate began to cause problems. Everyone else would be involved in an activity but Lisa would keep to the side, whispering in the corner with a friend. She would make fun of the teachers and the students who were participating. In class this undercurrent of sarcasm was disruptive, not just

★

because Lisa's mocking remarks would interrupt the flow of the class, but also because she would so frequently disappear. The teachers would have to look for her, often not finding her at all.

Sometimes they might have been secretly grateful that Lisa wasn't around. The belligerence was getting worse. A roughness and hostility were creeping into her manner as she refused to follow the teachers' directions.

Teachers speculated that Lisa's problems with the school might have been caused by an underlying resentment toward Scientology. For all they knew, the religion had been forced on her by her mother. Although Lisa later fully embraced the religion, now she seemed dissatisfied with this Scientology environment.

And there was trouble at home. According to one teacher, Lisa seemed neglected. The checks for school were always late. Priscilla was away a lot, working on the estate problems and developing her own career outside of Elvis' shadow. She was now a highly visible performer: hostess of *Those Amazing Animals,* the spokesperson for Wella Balsam shampoo, and a guest star on *Tony Orlando and Dawn.* Soon, she landed a starring role on *Dallas.*

Lisa never seemed to have any pocket money, always borrowing or scrounging off friends. She was literally a poor little rich girl. All in all, ac-

★

cording to one concerned teacher, "Lisa did not appear totally taken care of."

Despite their speculations, the teachers didn't know all that was really going on in Lisa's life. The financial troubles of her trust fund were just a part of the problem. While Priscilla was away, Mike Edwards had ceased trying to be a father figure—instead, he had fallen in love with Lisa!

He admits in his memoirs that he desired Lisa physically. Apparently, the sight of her glistening prepubescent teenage body was extremely tempting. Once when they were swimming together, he rubbed up against her wet skin. He became so aroused he had to force himself away from her to control his desire.

He began to flirt with Lisa. He took photographs of her by the pool, dressing her up in her mother's clothing, playing with her hair, giving her a rose, putting makeup on her, and marveling at how her body was developing. He told her how pretty she was. Edwards was so excited by these episodes that he confesses he wanted to make love to Lisa.

Finally, he crept into her bedroom while she was asleep. He just stared at her as she lay softly cuddled in her bed.

He realized he could no longer be around Lisa and contain his desires. His relationship with Priscilla suffered and Edwards moved to his

★

own apartment as their relationship slowly disintegrated.

Actually, Edwards' lust is hard to imagine. Lisa, still in her early teens, was not yet the beauty she would become. Like many early adolescents, she was slightly pudgy. Her body was ungainly and she had yet to shed her baby fat. But beauty is in the eye of the beholder, and Edwards' forbidden attraction resists anyone else's analysis. Elvis himself fell in love with Priscilla when she was but fourteen.

All that Lisa will say about these episodes, never referring to Edwards directly by name, is "that man . . . was sick."

Back at school, Lisa seemed more sullen. She spent all her time hanging out with the equally detached "cool crowd." Although they appeared to be clean-cut, they in fact had problems of their own.

To the horror and shock of the tightly knit Apple School community, one of these children died of a drug overdose. He was sniffing glue and went too far.

This boy had been a close friend of Lisa's. Teachers noticed the effect of his death on Lisa. Since she was always vulnerable to loss, it could only have added to her emotional confusion and misery, which expressed itself in increased hostility at school.

It was unclear whether her friend's death was

★

accidental or a deliberate suicide. In either case, the school was devastated.

The drug-related nature of the death was particularly unsettling. Scientology has a strong antidrug bias. In fact, this was one of the attractions of the faith for Priscilla. She herself had done the Purification Rundown, which set out to cleanse participants of all traces of drugs, alcohol, and radiation.

Despite the Apple School's avowed antidrug orientation, was this drug-related death an isolated incident? What exactly were Lisa and her "cool" friends up to? Were emotional problems alone the only cause of Lisa's increased moodiness and roughness? Or was something else involved?

Priscilla noticed the warning signs: perpetual sluggishness, a distant or distracted quality. And most telling, Lisa wouldn't look Priscilla in the eye. But when she did, Priscilla couldn't help but notice Lisa's dilated pupils.

The fact is, Lisa, who had been playing with dolls at Graceland only a few years before, had begun dabbling with drugs.

She started by experimenting with sedatives. (Interestingly, sedatives such as Quaaludes and Seconal were drugs her father often took.) Then Lisa moved on to marijuana, making a start on the path of drug problems that had ultimately doomed her father.

★

Drugs were a fact of life among the *jeunesse d'orée* of Beverly Hills. Growing up with entertainer parents who were preoccupied with their careers and often taking drugs themselves, these kids were acquainted with drugs early on. With large amounts of cash at home and lots of free time, it was natural for them to begin experimenting on their own.

Some, like Drew Barrymore, were by Lisa's age already recovering alcoholics who could only manage to take life one day at a time. Beginning drugs at age ten, Drew was soon a coke addict. At thirteen, she had already been through hard-core withdrawal and an inpatient rehabilitation program.

But Lisa, unlike many of these jaded Beverly Hills youths, had additional burdens beyond typical teenage boredom or parental neglect. She had suffered a loss that no one else had. Unlike the other children in Hollywood, she had lost her father . . . she had lost Elvis.

When friends pointed out that her father had died from drugs, Lisa chose to ignore them. She could not be reasoned with. Words alone could not convince her to stop.

The school could offer some help. The Apple School's way of dealing with drugs or other infractions of rules was to put the student in Ethics, an actual physical area of the school. There the student would not take regular classes. In-

★

stead the student would have to concentrate on his or her problem using Scientology techniques: one would have to admit and make amends for the infraction, and do things to demonstrate that the lesson was learned. Once this was done, the student could get out of Ethics and back to schoolwork. No physical punishment was involved.

While the school's strong antidrug environment no doubt temporarily worked for Lisa, she was not so easily subdued. Like her father, nothing could stop her, whether for better or worse.

As a nine-year-old who dealt with Vegas audiences, as an eleven-year-old who easily handled Michael Edwards' intrusions, this fourteen-year-old did what she wanted. Despite her mother's concern and the school's influence, Lisa was still in a defiant phase and was about to begin a full-blown adolescent rebellion.

FOURTEEN

LISA, THE REBEL

★──★

LISA WAS TO STAY AT THE APPLE SCHOOL FOR ONLY
another year and a half. Her manner was becoming more and more gruff and sour. She
seemed to want to spend as little time as possible at school.

While at school, Lisa grew very exclusive. She
didn't associate with just anyone, only with people she considered worth her time.

The press presented a completely different
picture of Lisa; they portrayed her as sweet and

unaffected. Newspaper accounts of this period describe her as blissfully innocent of what her last name meant. But in fact, a classmate paints another picture: "She knew exactly who she was and what she could get away with."

Her classmates recall how, once Lisa got her driver's license, she would fly into the school parking lot only moments before school began. The second school was over, she would roar out of the parking lot in her sporty Toyota Celica Supra, nearly knocking down those in her way.

Her exclusivity no doubt led her to grow particularly close to one other celebrity student, Meeno Peluce, the star of the TV show *Voyagers*. Just friends, the two took a trip to Spain together, where they were hounded by the press. Back home, they laughed as they told everyone how they had to disguise themselves to avoid being harassed by the media. No longer as sheltered and vulnerable, Lisa could easily handle the outside world. Still, this didn't mean Lisa could handle being trapped in school.

Although her father and her mother both earned high school diplomas, Lisa herself would never graduate from high school. She tried sampling other schools but school was just not for her. Looking back on it now, Lisa told *Life* magazine she's sorry she doesn't have "the Diploma" but says, "I knew I was either going to stay [in school] and die or I was going to have to

★

get out." And get out she did, only completing the tenth grade.

While still in the Apple School, she also began developing a new set of outside friends—Metal Heads. They were wealthy Beverly Hills brats who were involved in a drug culture and did not attend the Apple School. Bonded together by their love of Heavy Metal music, spiky shoes, dyed hair, and with their arrogant, druggy attitude, these kids were just the sort that Priscilla wanted Lisa to avoid.

Lisa was drawn to these Heavy Metalers. She shared their musical tastes. Her favorite metal bands included Aerosmith and D.I.O., bands that shocked and outraged many parents. Although she didn't go overboard, Lisa emulated this hard rock look. She had funky black boots and lots of Heavy Metal accessories.

It was not surprising that Elvis' daughter was attracted to rebels. Elvis, in his day, had been a rebel as well. His performances, which caused him to be dubbed "Elvis, the Pelvis," were condemned by moralists. His long hair, his wild moves, his sexually charged performances and even rock 'n' roll itself, scandalized the public.

But Elvis' rebellion was essentially innocent. Extremely devoted to his parents, he still lived at home and his idea of fun was playing crack the whip at the roller rink.

Lisa's rebellion, on the other hand, was much

★

less innocent than her father's. While not a performer, she would attend concerts of bands whose lyrics were devoted to suicide and devil worship. She and her friends were interested in a subterranean scene that celebrated violence and Satanism.

Her fights with her mother were becoming more bitter. When Lisa turned sixteen, Priscilla imposed a ten o'clock curfew. But the day Lisa got her driver's license, she immediately drove away and did not return home or call that night. Priscilla was frantic. Lisa apologized. But the hostilities were far from over.

She would try to sneak away from home when her mother wasn't focused on her. Once, garishly dressed in very short shorts and wearing tons of lipstick and eye shadow, Lisa disappeared from the house. She was off to see some boy she was interested in.

But Priscilla was used to Lisa's tricks. She was not so easily fooled and followed her. Priscilla caught up with Lisa en route to her boyfriend's and insisted Lisa get in her car immediately. Lisa complied—this time.

Priscilla and Lisa took a trip to visit Edwards' family in Florida. Priscilla let Lisa go out dancing with Edwards' daughter Caroline and Caroline's boyfriend, but only on the condition that they all get home before midnight and that there be no drinking. At about midnight Lisa

★

called Priscilla, who was staying with Edwards' mother. Lisa told her mother that they were home safe.

In truth, Lisa made the call from a bar. They had been drinking. Things turned ugly when Caroline's boyfriend slapped Caroline in the middle of a spat. Lisa jumped to her friend's defense.

Puffed up, Lisa threatened the boyfriend. "I have the power and money to ruin you." (Sweet and unaffected? Unaware of who her father was? Lisa was obviously less naive than the newspapers claimed.)

Their drunken fun shattered by the fight, Lisa and Caroline left the bar.

They returned home and found to their dismay that Priscilla was on her way over. She'd guessed that Lisa had been lying because of the background noise she'd heard during the call.

When Priscilla arrived, she was seething with rage. According to Edwards, she slapped Caroline and then quickly struck Lisa in the face. Lisa tried to run, but Edwards stopped her as Priscilla caught her by her hair.

Priscilla pulled Lisa into the Cadillac in the driveway. On the back seat, she began to spank Lisa, who yelled. Priscilla tried to cover Lisa's mouth to keep her quiet.

The police were attracted by all the screaming and shouting. They drove up in a patrol car

★

and got out to investigate. Somehow Priscilla managed to get rid of them and mother and daughter left for Beverly Hills the next morning.

Back in Beverly Hills, this sixteen-year-old could not be fully tamed. Once a tiny terror on her golf cart, Lisa now had her car to play with. When she was angry and didn't feel like coming home and facing her mother, Lisa would just sleep in her car. Once, according to friends, she did this for three days straight. Her mother would take her car away but then she would give it back and the cycle would continue.

Rebellious Lisa, like any teenager, needed to break free from her mother. She was trying to form her own identity, independent from a mother who was particularly protective. But Lisa still needed love. She thought she'd found it in the person of her first serious boyfriend.

Lisa began dating him in her early teens, when he was about eighteen. He immediately made a good impression on the family, convincing Priscilla, Lisa, and even Mike Edwards of his sincerity and charm.

Polite and exuberant, he was everything a parent could want in a boyfriend. Edwards would chaperone their dates and the boy always seemed the perfect gentleman. How relieved Priscilla must have been to find that her daughter was not dating one of the Metal Heads.

★

Innocently, the young couple would kiss and cuddle in the back seat as the chaperone drove them home from a date. At last Lisa had found someone she could trust and of whom her mother would approve. Here was someone who was interested in Lisa for herself, and not for her famous last name. Or so she thought.

They had been going out for three years when he lured her into a park where a photographer was waiting. Suddenly, Lisa found pictures of their private day alone in a magazine. He had sold them to the press. The boyfriend that she was so devoted to was just another gold digger, ready to capitalize on her famous name.

Priscilla's lifelong effort to protect Lisa and shield her from the press had been sabotaged. Everything Priscilla had tried to prevent had happened.

Lisa had trouble accepting what her boyfriend had done. Even though he had betrayed her, she could not automatically turn off her feelings for him. Lisa seemed more hurt and confused than angry.

For underneath her recently acquired tough exterior, Lisa was still a very sensitive, easily wounded young girl. She was extremely vulnerable to loss. It had only been six years since her father died, six years of financial and personal upheavals. Her life had been marked by her parents' painful divorce, Elvis' tragic death, her

★

mother's changing boyfriends, the radically different environments of Beverly Hills and Memphis, the threat of financial ruin, a kaleidoscope of different schools, exposure to drugs and drinking, the constant fear of the press, and now exploitation by her boyfriend. Lisa had faced all these already and she was only sixteen.

According to her mother, the experience with this boyfriend, "set Lisa back a couple of years." Her mother's wariness and caution had been justified all along. But Lisa could not acknowledge this yet. If anything, it must have been more important now than ever for her to prove that she was her own person, independent from her mother. Vulnerable and wounded, her drug problems and wildness increased.

Her Beverly Hills Heavy Metal friends were out there, waiting for her. Before ninth grade, Lisa had only experimented with pot and sedatives. Now, away from the Apple School, alienated from her mother, and back with the Metal Heads, Lisa began trying harder drugs—she became seriously involved with cocaine.

It was clear where Lisa was headed. Something had to be done for her. As she had before, Priscilla again turned to Scientology for help.

FIFTEEN

THE CELEBRITY CENTRE

★─────────────────────────────────────★

SCIENTOLOGY IS A RELIGION FOUNDED BY THE SCI-
ence fiction writer L. Ron Hubbard in the 1950's.
It is devoted to improving the quality of its follower's lives through the use of procedures developed by L. Ron Hubbard.

Central to its beliefs is a method of counseling
called auditing. Auditing sessions often use an
"E meter"—actually a modified galvonometer—
which like a lie detector registers electrical
changes in the skin. An individual undergoing

★

auditing is asked questions and the E meter registers emotional responses, which are then analyzed. The goal of the sessions is to help eradicate "engrams"—negative mental imprints. Once this is fully accomplished, the church member is declared "clear"—in complete control of his or her thought processes.

Critics of Scientology have described it as a cult. Its detractors have branded the religion a money-making scheme devised by its founder. Auditing can be extremely expensive, costing up to hundreds of dollars a session. L. Ron is on record as saying "If a man really wants to make a million dollars, the best way would be to start his own religion."

According to former church members, Scientology, at its height in the 1970's, had assets of three hundred million dollars.

L. Ron Hubbard shrouded himself in secrecy. For years he ran the church from his yacht, *The Apollo,* reportedly surrounded by a group of young followers who had only been educated in his teachings. This core of teenagers, dressed in nautical garb, was called the Commodore's Messenger Organization and, according to Scientology dissidents, gradually took over the church. For a long time, L. Ron did not appear in public and many speculated that he was dead or being held captive by the elite guard he had established.

★

In 1982 his son instigated a lawsuit to have L. Ron declared dead or mentally incompetent because L. Ron had not been seen in public for many years. L. Ron was alive, however. He died peacefully in 1986 in California aboard the motor home where he resided. There were numerous other lawsuits against the church. Some of the most important legal battles were with the IRS.

The tax status of Scientology and of Scientologists' payments to Scientology were questioned by the IRS. In 1984, the U.S. Tax Court decided that the mother Scientology church in California did not qualify as a tax-exempt religious organization under the Internal Revenue Code for the years 1970 through 1972. The Tax Court found that the church had diverted profits to its founder and others, had conspired to impede collection of its taxes, and had conducted almost all activities for a commercial purpose. An appeal followed, and, in 1987, the federal Court of Appeals that decides appeals of federal cases in California affirmed the Tax Court. (The Appeals Court based its decision solely on the ground that the Church had diverted profits for the use of private individuals without addressing the other bases of the Tax Court's decision.) In 1989, in another group of cases involving Scientology, the U.S. Supreme Court decided that payments made by Scientologists to branch

★

churches were not tax deductible charitable contributions because they were more like a payment for services than the type of gift that qualifies as a tax deductible contribution.

Despite these controversies, even those who have left the church speak of its effectiveness in combating drug addiction.

This antidrug attitude was, according to friends, an important consideration in Priscilla's decision to place Lisa in a Scientology facility in Los Angeles called the Celebrity Centre. The Celebrity Centre is located on Franklin Avenue in Hollywood. The building was once a French Normandy-style luxury hotel that in its heyday housed such stars as Humphrey Bogart, Edward G. Robinson, Gable and Lombard, Errol Flynn, and Ginger Rogers. But it had fallen on hard times. In 1973, the church purchased the hotel and renovated it back to its former sumptuous state.

A social facility and a site for Scientology classes and auditing sessions, the Celebrity Centre is also an apartment building. Both celebrity and noncelebrity members of the church can live there as long as they are "on course"—continuing one's study. Scientology does indeed boast many celebrity members, including Chick Corea, John Travolta, Karen Black, and Kirstie Alley. But when Lisa Marie Presley moved into the Celebrity Centre, all attention was on her.

★

Lisa did not make the best first impression. Everyone assumed she was snobby and arrogant because she kept to herself and never spoke. Many remembered her from her days at the Apple School and how exclusive and belligerent she had been. Although not in any way hostile to the other residents of the CC (Celebrity Centre), she was very quiet and didn't seem to notice or care about the Scientologists there who were her own age.

Everyone knew why she was there: her mother had put her there to keep her away from drugs. But even in the drug-free environment of the Celebrity Centre, when Lisa first moved in she still kept up with her old set of friends from the wild days—the Metal Heads.

The Heavy Metalers were an odd sight in the clean-cut Celebrity Centre. They would stroll in, wearing their heavy metal garb and sporting long, spiky haircuts, and make their way to visit Lisa upstairs. Lisa, herself, waiting in her room, fit right in, wearing tight pants and copying their attitude. The only difference was that Lisa's hair was neither spiky nor dyed, but straight and still its natural honey-blond.

Lisa's spacious apartment was located on one of the upper floors of the Celebrity Centre. Many in the Celebrity Centre slept five or six in a room, but Lisa could afford private accommodations. Although the furniture was very simple,

★

no expense was spared in housing the daughter of the King. Lisa's room was larger than most, with lots of windows, lavender walls, and new charcoal-gray carpeting. She had a TV and a stereo. Significantly, there were no pictures of Elvis or Priscilla.

Once the Metalers were in her room, the door would be slammed shut. Knowing that no one knew what they were up to, the parties, even in the drug-free environment of the Celebrity Centre, grew wilder, even though Lisa was trying to become drug-free and "clear."

This Heavy Metal crowd was disregarding the rules of the Celebrity Centre. They weren't even supposed to be there—Lisa wasn't allowed to have anybody in her apartment.

Priscilla somehow got wind of what Lisa was up to. One time when a couple of long-haired guys and a girl were partying in her apartment, her mom called. "God, it's my mom. You've got to leave." The fun had ended and Lisa was furious.

As the Metal Heads left, taking their druggy atmosphere right out of the door with them, all Lisa could say was, "I hate my mom." Like any teenager, she was still rebellious and resentful when her freedoms were curtailed by her mother.

But the fact is, deep in her heart, Lisa knew her mother was right—drugs were contrary to

★

her own best interests. Lisa realized this most clearly one night when things went too far.

Lisa hadn't slept in three days—a three-day party in which she was kept wired by cocaine. She was with about half a dozen friends who were still getting high. Lisa could either do more coke and remain high or end the party, get some sleep, and try to lead a normal life.

Lisa flushed the coke down the toilet.

Although no one else knew it, her involvement with drugs had ended.

Lisa was going to try to follow the rules of the Celebrity Centre and struggle to remain drug-free. This dark chapter in her life, one that had caused so many problems with her mother, drew to a close and now she and Priscilla could begin to mend the rift between them.

Lisa, committed to the Celebrity Centre and living by its precepts, was ready for a new group of friends. Until this point, she hadn't fully integrated into the group of other youthful residents of the CC. They found her intriguing.

Who was this aloof, frosty girl who kept to herself except for visits from Heavy Metal friends? Lisa was the same age as the young Scientologists but her life had clearly been so different from any of theirs. Finally, their curiosity got the better of them, and they found the courage to approach her, assuming she'd be unfriendly and imperious.

★

But to their surprise, Lisa was friendly. Those who had talked to her would excitedly report to other friends that "Lisa's nice . . . She's a nice girl." The girl who had been so exclusive and unfriendly at the Apple School had changed. She'd been through a lot and after a year in the Celebrity Centre, she was finally growing up. The reserved exterior was not an indication of a haughty desire to remain apart, but of Lisa's shyness.

Every day she was trying to fit more into life at the Celebrity Centre. Aside from auditing, Lisa was taking Scientology courses such as one called Student's Hat: a course in how to be a student. It emphasized such Scientology concepts as Misunderstood Words. Priscilla herself was also often at the Celebrity Centre studying Scientology, furthering the reconciliation process between mother and daughter.

The metal friends were gone; Lisa had exorcised them from her life. Even her look had changed. Gone were the tight pants and the Heavy Metal accessories. Lisa was now more conventionally dressed. Someone who was a resident at the time remarks that while Lisa had more clothes than most teens, she can only picture Lisa wearing boxer shorts and a halter top. Her more clean-cut look mirrored her change in companions.

Once the ice was broken, Lisa was a warm

★

friend. For example, she would give you a ride home if you needed one. She judged you on your own merits, not by how much money your parents had or whether they were famous. Lisa was a real friend to Leslie Prickert, Sammie Basso, and another girl named Lisa—her new set of pals.

Unlike the Metal Heads, Lisa now had a group she could bring home, one her mom would welcome. Lisa gave a party for her new Scientology friends at Priscilla's Beverly Hills home.

Lisa at this time in her life rarely talked about Elvis. Difficult as it was, she was trying to forge ahead rather than concentrating on the past. But this evening was different. She showed her friends mementos and precious reminders of her father—his army jacket, his sunglasses, and family pictures.

Lisa, more at peace with herself and her legacy, was now able to share her memories of her father.

Back in Memphis, all that Elvis had wanted her to have and remember him by had in the end been rescued. His gestures of love had not been made in vain. The estate he had left to her had not gone bankrupt. Graceland had been saved.

Imaginatively, Priscilla and her advisers

thought up the idea of opening Graceland to the public. It would be run as a tourist attraction, like other historic homes such as the Hearst Castle.

This way the estate could solve its financial problems, the fans would finally be able to get inside Elvis' home, and most importantly, Graceland would be kept for Lisa.

Lisa could come back whenever she wanted. Everything would be kept exactly as it was to the point where Priscilla could say, "If Lisa wanted to move in . . . she could go in with a toothbrush and that's it."

Now, fans filtered through, but only during the day. The twelve dollars they spent on an average visit all went to help maintain Graceland and provide for Lisa. Whether the fans knew it or not, most of the gift shops across the street were also owned by Lisa's trust fund; money spent here also went into her pocket.

Through these measures, the dire financial situation had been quickly reversed. Graceland became a profit-making enterprise, grossing $6 million a year. The home her father had loved and wanted her to have was saved. Thanks to clever management, the King's Princess was not going to end up a pauper.

* * *

★

Elvis would no doubt have been happy that Lisa was so well provided for and, under the church's guidance, was beginning to get her life together.

Yet Elvis himself had always been very suspicious of Scientology. According to his spiritual adviser, Larry Geller, Elvis believed that Scientologists were deceptive and dangerous. He told Larry, "They never mention God. They just want me. They want my name and my money. *That's* what they're into."

What would his response have been if he had learned that his daughter was not only involved with this religion, but also had attended its schools and was living in one of its centers?

Lisa's progress was undeniable, but if Elvis had been alive, would he have allowed Lisa to plunge into Scientology? . . . Would it even have been necessary?

SIXTEEN

D-BAT

★————————————————————————★

EVEN THOUGH LISA HAD OPENED UP TO OTHERS, shedding her self-protective arrogance and becoming much friendlier, she still wasn't Miss Sugary Sweet.

She continued to talk tough. "Get out of my face," she'd say to one friend, or, "What the hell do you think you're doing?" to another. But now Lisa's smile made it clear she was joking or being sarcastic rather than belligerent.

At the Celebrity Centre, a group of guys ap-

★

preciated Lisa's attitude and her style. They too were tough but also quite sincere. They were the members of a band that was the center of attention for teen-scene Scientologists—D-BAT. With their pop rock, top-forty style, D-BAT struck a chord within the Scientology community. Whenever they played at the Celebrity Centre, there was a frenzy of excitement—they were hot! And one member of D-BAT would change Lisa's life.

D-BAT stands for *D*anny, *B*ooth, *A*lex, and *T*had, the four members of the band. Alex was the lead singer, and Derek Booth was another singer. The band was founded by its drummer, Thad Corea, son of the well-known jazz great Chick Corea. Danny Keough was the bass player. Everyone except for Derek had his own motorcycle.

Like the Metal Heads, their lives revolved around music. But there was one crucial difference—D-BAT was drug-free. But they were hardly tame!

The band would cruise around Los Angeles on their motorcycles, a veritable Scientology motorcycle gang: clean-cut youths gunning their big bikes down Hollywood Boulevard. No one knew who they were but everyone noticed these bikers roaring along the boulevards of Los Angeles and pouring in and out of clubs.

Lisa would accompany them on their noctur-

★

nal outings, her arms clinging around the waist of whichever biker was driving her that night. After a full day of auditing and Student's Hat, they would set out for the strip. Part of the L.A. night scene, they sampled the music at different clubs. Drinking was limited. They were underage, but more importantly they were Scientologists—they never went overboard. When the clubs were closing, they'd board their cycles and head for their habitual hangout—Canters.

Canters is a New York-style deli in West Hollywood that's famous for being open twenty-four hours a day, seven days a week. It's an unpretentious restaurant where you can order a simple hamburger and a Coke with fries. It's the sort of place that attracts a wide mix of people—celebrities like Emma Samms and Shelley Winters, older neighborhood residents, passing truck drivers, hot young agents, and even a Scientology motorcycle gang . . . accompanied by the daughter of the King.

Sometimes, Lisa and the gang would go to the glittery Hard Rock Cafe, but really Canters was more to their liking. For her and her friends, trendy, pretentious restaurants on Melrose or in Beverly Hills were not what D-BAT was all about.

And that's not what Lisa was all about. Most of her Beverly Hills contemporaries could be found at, say, the Westlake School for Girls,

★

cramming to get into an Ivy League college and learning about accessories, or spending the day as teen matrons, compulsively shopping, lunching, and dieting.

Lisa, on the other hand, was traveling on the back of motorcycles, devotedly following D-BAT, prowling through L.A. nightclubs, and eating her meals in all-night diners. Like Elvis, her tastes were simple but her appetite for fun was great. You could take the girl out of Memphis, but you couldn't make Lisa into a spoiled Beverly Hills teen sophisticate.

Lisa's life in the Celebrity Centre reinforced her unpretentiousness. Most people there came from ordinary backgrounds. And most of them now had average jobs, often in Scientology-connected businesses. Danny, for example, worked as a housepainter and on construction jobs, living with friends but always moving around a lot. Others, like Thad Corea, even if they had celebrity parents, still lived more or less like everyone else.

Despite the differences in their backgrounds, their lives had a common focus—Scientology. Most of the gang had gone to Scientology high schools—Lisa, the Apple School, and Danny and Alex, the Delphian School in Oregon. A friend who was living in the centre with them said, "Scientology was definitely there for us. It was part of our lives, but it wasn't taking over them.

★

We were serious about it, but we were only typical teenagers." Teenagers yes, typical no.

After all, they were living in a centre belonging to what many people consider one of the largest cults in the world. Beyond basic auditing, one could take more advanced courses in Scientology beliefs. Bent Corydon, in his book *L. Ron Hubbard: Messiah or Madman?*, co-authored with L. Ron's estranged son L. Ron Hubbard, Jr., describes some of these beliefs. Corydon alleges that the most advanced Scientology materials deal with immortality and parallel universes with a Galactic Confederation of Planets once ruled by a leader named Xenu who dispatched people to earth. This was hardly a conventional religion.

It was the Scientology Celebrity Centre that was most supportive of the band. It was here that they played almost all their gigs and it was here that they were stars. They would perform in the lobby for church functions.

But they also had an occasional gig outside of the CC. Sometimes D-BAT played at the Wine Room, a Greek restaurant across the street.

The rest of their time was spent practicing and recording in the studio. They were hungry for a record contract, hoping to be picked up and signed by a major label. Lisa would hang out with D-BAT, but never performed with them.

★

Even though the tabloids often report that Lisa has a great voice, those who know her well never mention that she's a singer. For the members of the band, it was never assumed that Lisa was a singer just because her father was. In fact her mother has indicated that Lisa's gift lies as a lyricist. Perhaps Lisa's love of music will someday express itself in this way.

But at the time, rather than writing music, Lisa was content to listen to D-BAT. As her devotion to the band grew, so did her interest in one member—Danny Keough.

★

SEVENTEEN

DANNY

★──★

OF ALL THE MEMBERS OF D-BAT, DANNY, AL-
though not the lead singer, was the one who
stood out. Confident and outgoing, he combined
gregariousness and warmth with a very real talent. He was a serious musician, devoted to his
bass playing and to the band.

Born in 1964, Danny grew up in Oregon. His
mother, Janet, and his stepfather, Alan Hol-
lander, were Scientology educators with a modest life-style. They co-founded the Delphian

School from which Danny graduated. He moved to L.A. in 1984, and began to work at odd jobs while pursuing his musical career. Aside from playing with D-BAT he did an occasional gig at Mad Hatter Studios, which belonged to fellow Scientologist and jazz great Chick Corea.

Although he didn't live at the Celebrity Centre, he certainly spent a lot of time there, visiting his best friend, Thad Corea, who was also in the band. While not the leader of his group of friends, Danny was extremely popular. Friends remember him as being "really, really nice."

Others who knew the handsome six-footer are more critical. "He was really conceited," an ex-girlfriend says. "He couldn't speak well and sounded uneducated. His grammar was poor. But he was streetsmart."

Perhaps this made him even more appealing to Lisa, who was also not booksmart, but knew the ways of the world. Not intellectuals, Danny and Lisa both were streetwise, and both used blunt, tough language.

While girls were always attracted to Danny, at first he and Lisa were only friends. He already had a longtime girlfriend—another Scientologist—named Suzy.

But even though Danny and Suzy had been going out for a while, he was not a one-woman man. He had brief flings or even one-night stands, but Suzy was the one he kept around

★

most. They certainly had been through a lot together.

One night, the band was driving back to the Celebrity Centre from Canters on their motorcycles. Danny was behind everybody with Suzy holding tightly onto him. Suddenly, Danny lost control of the motorcycle on a turn. It toppled over and over and skidded along the pavement, eventually coming to a halt with a crunch. The battered cycle ended up under a van parked by the side of the road. Danny was lucky—he was unharmed and walked away from the accident. Suzy was not so lucky. She had to be hospitalized.

While Danny was still going out with Suzy, he saw Lisa a lot. They were part of the same group of friends. But he never said much about her to his friends or revealed any special feelings for her. This is partially because of the CC taboo against talking about people behind their backs. Actually, most of his conversation consisted of talking about the band and their dreams of rock glory.

Lisa, however, could not be completely ignored. Not just because she was always with the band, not just because she was Elvis' daughter, but because of her juicy personality . . . and her juicy looks. Still, it took time for each of them to realize how attracted to one another they actually were.

★

Lisa and Danny and a few other friends spent a lot of nights hanging out in Lisa's room, watching TV. It was always a relaxed evening. They wouldn't rent movies, but were content to watch whatever programs happened to be on. Lisa would never serve any food or alcohol; she wasn't particularly domestic and drinking wasn't really allowed.

Danny was always the liveliest one, cracking jokes and making fun of the shows to everyone's amusement. Lisa usually just sat there and laughed along. Typically, she was very quiet during these evenings, rarely making any jokes of her own, even though she was among her closest friends.

The evening would wind down and gradually everyone would make their exit back to their own rooms. Soon, only Lisa, her good friend Sammie Basso, and Danny would be left. Then Sammie would leave.

Clearly, romance was brewing.

Before long, Danny and Lisa were casually dating, seeing each other alone or with friends at concerts, Canters, or Scientology functions.

But then it became clear that this was not another of Danny's casual flings nor a diversion for bored Lisa. Around the CC, they could be seen holding hands or walking arm and arm, oblivious to the rest of the world. They would cuddle together on the sofa while watching TV,

★

a certain gleam in their eyes that they could hide from no one.

Lisa and Danny had fallen in love!

Here was the person that Lisa had always wanted, had always needed. This was a man she could respect. In his small circle, he was a famous musician, doing what he loved best. He was a virtuous Scientologist, but not in an overbearing way. He was secure in who he was and in his love for Lisa. "Danny is his own man—not trying to be Elvis," Lisa told the press. He and Lisa were meant for each other.

One night they went to a party in the rambling Hollywood Hills home of a fellow Scientologist. They held hands as they walked in the door, presenting to the other guests the image of a happy young couple very much in love.

But standing right in front of them was one of Danny's old girlfriends, a beautiful girl with whom he had had a very intimate relationship, a fact of which Lisa was no doubt aware. The moment was incredibly tense. The three of them had shared a passionate history.

Danny politely acknowledged his ex-lover's presence with a friendly hello. Lisa, however, just smirked. According to the ex-girlfriend, Lisa radiated condescension. Lisa felt so secure in her relationship with Danny that it bordered on smugness. She seemed to be saying, "Danny

★

and I have got each other and we're mature enough to not care at all about what happened between you and Danny in the past."

She got her comeuppance when, according to a follower of D-BAT, Danny briefly revived his relationship with his other old girlfriend, Suzy. They began seeing each other again after he had been involved with Lisa. But this renewed relationship was short-lived—Lisa was the one for him.

And he remained the one for her. Unlike her first love who betrayed her at a tender age, Danny showed no signs of being interested in her for her name and her money. As his closest friends say emphatically, "Danny a gold digger? —No way! No way!"

Lisa herself needed to be cautious of gold diggers more than ever because her trust fund had grown so enormously. Under Priscilla's inspired guidance, Graceland had been turned into a veritable gold mine. From near bankruptcy, Lisa's trust fund was now worth close to $100 million.

This didn't mean Lisa was spoiled. Priscilla was determined to teach Lisa the value of money.

Lisa began a job in an office. According to an unconfirmed rumor reported by the Baroness Alina Morini, Lisa worked in a Los Angeles travel agency linked to the Church of

★

Scientology. Lisa told *Life* magazine, "I had this normal-type entry level job, ten to five, just like anybody else." Lisa's ignorance of the expression *"nine* to five" indicates that she is not "just like anybody else."

Danny was working too, continuing with construction and housepainting. Unfortunately, D-BAT was breaking up. According to a friend of the band, "they were very talented but they weren't all willing to put in the effort." Derek moved back to England but Danny and Thad remained close.

Priscilla as one of the executors of the trust began to involve Lisa with the estate, explaining to her how the business was run.

Priscilla knew that on the horizon was the fact that Lisa would gain control of her trust when she turned twenty-five. The executors however, with Lisa's consent, made a controversial move in the summer of 1988. They extended the trust for an additional five years, when Lisa will turn thirty. Things were going so well that they decided to stick with what had worked. Why make any changes?

The tabloids screamed that Priscilla was stealing Lisa's money. This, of course, was not true as Lisa's estate is held in a closely watched trust. Priscilla has not taken any of the capital of the trust and when the additional period is over all the money will be Lisa's.

★

However, the executors have profited from the trust. In 1982 the executors billed the trust $240,000 for their services. But more importantly, Priscilla, as an executor of the trust, though divorced from Elvis and left nothing in his will, reestablished her links to Elvis. She even now oversees a TV series about her former husband.

When Lisa and Priscilla together announced their decision about the management plans of the estate, no traces of the turbulent past remained. Mother and daughter were no longer merely close . . . they were now best friends.

Lisa was also fond of Priscilla's new boyfriend, Marco Garibaldi, a Brazilian screenwriter. Priscilla had begun seeing Marco after Mike Edwards left.

At first, Priscilla had been reluctant to introduce her new boyfriend to Lisa. She and Marco had been seeing each other for two months when Lisa took action. One day she saw Marco's car in the driveway and demanded to meet him. Fortunately, everyone hit it off. He was by far Lisa's favorite among all her mother's boyfriends and Priscilla was very much in love with him.

Years ago, Priscilla told *Ladies' Home Journal* that she would never have more children after Lisa. "I don't think it would be fair to the other children, if Elvis wasn't their father, too."

★

But Priscilla apparently overcame these reservations when she became pregnant with Marco's child.

The pregnancy tightened the bond between mother and daughter. They attended Lamaze classes together and Lisa was present at the birth of her half-brother, Navarone, in April of 1986. Lisa immediately fell in love with her little half-brother.

Priscilla was so proud of her new child and her wonderful new relationship with Lisa. It seemed as if the rocky times were far behind them, soon to become only distant memories.

Mother and daughter even made a TV commercial together that made fun of their past problems and Priscilla's strictness. The commercial puns on what Priscilla would "put her foot down" on: Lisa's new hairdos, new boyfriends, and . . . an Oldsmobile accelerator.

For this commercial, Lisa and Priscilla earned $250,000 plus a new car. It was Lisa's first venture into show business since her days in the spotlight during Elvis' performances in Vegas.

Priscilla must have been so pleased with how her daughter's life was proceeding: Lisa was a devout Scientologist, involved in a stable relationship with a young man who loved her and treated her right, free from drugs, and finally at peace with her father's legacy. Lisa was the

★

very emblem of someone who was in control of her life.

Then one day, Lisa made an announcement to her mother that took Priscilla completely by surprise.

"Mom, you know, I'm pregnant."

EIGHTEEN

Happily Ever After?

★———————————————————★

PRISCILLA WAS SHOCKED WHEN LISA TOLD HER SHE was pregnant. Just when things had been going so smoothly for Lisa, this complication occurred. Priscilla admits, "Every emotion hit me at the same time. I was anxious and even angry."

Was this the same ambivalence and uncertainty Priscilla had felt about her own pregnancy with Lisa? Priscilla had been a young wife just married to Elvis when she found that

★

she was carrying a child. She questioned whether she and Elvis were ready for this sudden change in their lives. They were settled in every other respect, but she could not be certain what a new, unplanned baby would mean.

Lisa, on the other hand, was not the slightest bit settled. As Priscilla said in an interview, Lisa still had too many "undone factors" in her life. Although for the first time Lisa was on an even keel, she had not finished high school, only recently gotten off drugs, and hadn't decided on a career. She wasn't even married. Was she really ready to have a baby?

Therefore, Lisa had many more reasons to feel ambivalent about having her baby than the young Priscilla did about having Lisa. Priscilla had even considered aborting Lisa. Lisa, by comparison, projected an image of total happiness and deep commitment to her unborn child. Her love for Danny and their baby was all that mattered. A spokesperson at Graceland described Lisa as "just ecstatic."

Priscilla was eventually won over. She couldn't forget how enthusiastic Lisa had been about her pregnancy with Navarone. And Lisa was such a help when it came to raising him. Priscilla came to understand that Lisa knew what having a child entailed. Priscilla has said, "I came to realize that Lisa and her husband

★

felt they were ready and that they were willing to take on the responsibility."

A wedding was decided on.

It would be held at the Celebrity Centre. Although they were no longer living at the CC, but were sharing a house with Scientology friends, the location meant so much to Danny and Lisa. It was at the Celebrity Centre that Lisa had clarified her life, it was where they had met, and it was where their romance had begun.

On the afternoon of October 3, 1988, they tied the knot. Lisa was a beautiful bride, clad in a dusty-rose knee-length silk gown. Danny, wearing a conservative dark suit, beamed with pride. Here were two young people, like Elvis and Priscilla years before, in love with each other and completely committed to their lives together.

Reverend Sarah Gualtieri of the Church of Scientology joined them together. For seven minutes Lisa and Danny exchanged vows as they were united in matrimony.

Priscilla looked on, overflowing with emotion. She cried tears of joy and also tears of sadness, for she was losing her little girl. She was accompanied by her sister Michelle and her parents, who had missed Priscilla's wedding in Vegas. In all, there were only nine guests present. Three generations of beautiful Beaulieu women gathered together to witness the marriage of the youngest, who would soon bring forth a new life.

As their vows were completed, bathed in the love of everyone present, Danny and Lisa were pronounced husband and wife.

Unlike at Elvis and Priscilla's wedding, no members of the press were present. Once again, Priscilla had kept cleverly Lisa hidden. The veil of secrecy that Elvis and Priscilla had maintained for Lisa since her birth was still in place. When the press finally got wind of the event two days later, it was too late: Lisa and Danny were gone.

They had left for a three-month secret honeymoon.

Priscilla's publicist would not reveal the location. Later, Priscilla disclosed to *Life* magazine that Lisa and Danny had been on a yacht in the Caribbean. What she didn't admit was that Lisa was aboard the *Freewinds,* the Scientology yacht.

The *Freewinds* was not the Church's first yacht. Another ship—the *Apollo*—had once served as L. Ron Hubbard's mobile headquarters. The *Apollo* was the source of some controversy—Bent Corydon, in *L. Ron Hubbard: Messiah or Madman,* alleged that Hubbard and his followers had engaged in strange activities on the ship. The *Apollo* was later sold and converted into a floating restaurant.

★

Despite such allegations, however, Lisa's trip on the Scientology yacht *Freewinds* was only marred by morning sickness.

Lisa had to leave the ship before the three-month honeymoon was over, according to many reports, and headed for Venezuela to keep out of the eye of the press. Then, with only a few months left before the due date, Danny and Lisa returned to L.A.

Lisa did not return to her job. Nor did she pursue any more commercial or TV work. Any talked-about plans to finish high school through correspondence classes had to be put off. All Lisa's attention was focused on the impending birth.

Priscilla was also eagerly awaiting Lisa's baby, her first grandchild. She was actively involved in Lisa's life during these final months. This did not mean that Priscilla controlled Lisa or was an overbearing mother-in-law. Lisa and Priscilla's relationship, although extremely complex, was very loving. Mother/daughter roles were often reversed.

For instance, Priscilla controlled the family finances, but it was Lisa's money and Lisa's alone. Priscilla tried to shield Lisa from the press, but Lisa tried to shield Priscilla from the harshness of the real world, forbidding Priscilla to watch upsetting stories on the evening news. Priscilla went to pieces over Baby Jessica's

★

plight in the well and Lisa was determined not to let Priscilla break down that way again. It could almost be said that each was overprotective of the other.

Lisa and Priscilla had taken Lamaze classes together before, and now Lisa and Danny shared this bonding experience. Lisa's protective instincts were now focused on her baby.

The Lamaze technique emphasizes birth without fear through knowledge of the birthing process. The husband's role is vital. It is he who can assist his wife the most, aiding her both physically and emotionally.

Together, Lisa and Danny would practice for the birth, learning the Lamaze breathing techniques. Panting, followed by deep, slow breaths as well as the physical actions of pushing, would all be used in order to take the mother's mind off the pain of birth, making delivery easier.

The husband is intimately involved with the final stages of pregnancy. Once the mother goes into labor, the father massages her tense body to keep it calm. As hard labor begins and delivery is imminent, he can bring her chips of ice to cool her.

The father is present during the actual delivery. He is allowed to cut the umbilical cord and catch the newborn baby.

Through these Lamaze techniques, delivery

★

can be a less painful, more holistic, and shared experience.

As the days dwindled down to what is truly a miraculous event, Lisa and Danny drew closer and closer. They practiced for hours together, thrilled and perhaps a little nervous about the impending birth.

On the last weekend in May 1989, Lisa finally went into labor. She was rushed to Saint John's Hospital in Santa Monica at 2:30 in the morning on May 29th.

Danny was by her side in the hospital.

But Lisa and Danny were not alone in their joyous anticipation. The entire world was waiting for the birth of Elvis Presley's first grandchild. The only question was—who would Lisa name it after . . . Elvis or L. Ron?

NINETEEN

ELVIS LIVES!

★————————————————————————————————★

AT 8:15 P.M., ON MONDAY, MAY 29, 1989, LISA brought forth baby Danielle.

This beautiful seven-pound, two-ounce baby girl confounded all predictions by being given the feminized version of her father Danny's name: Danielle. Dr. Moran, the obstetrician, through a hospital spokesperson, told the press that it was "an easy birth, no complications."

Just as during Lisa's own birth in Baptist Memorial Hospital in Memphis, security was tight.

★

The press was kept at a distance, but they stalked Saint John's Hospital relentlessly.

Although Elvis' plan to trick the press when Priscilla was brought to the hospital failed, Lisa and Danny proved to be more clever at hiding themselves. Some speculated that she was actually giving birth in Phoenix, Arizona, while others believed that Lisa had made a hasty nighttime exit from the hospital in a jeep to avoid the onslaught of reporters.

The confusion was settled when one photographer, Cezarre Bono, was brought in for a ten-minute shoot of the happy family, with Lisa holding the one-day-old Danielle. The photo would end up on the cover of *People* magazine, making Danielle the youngest celebrity ever to get a *People* cover.

Grandma Priscilla visited Lisa and the baby soon after the birth. According to Great-grandfather Joseph Beaulieu, "She's always bubbly and she's just more so now." Lisa and Danny glowed with pride at having brought forth this child into the world.

Elvis would have been so proud. The newborn babe whom twenty-one years ago he'd carried across the halls of Graceland to present to Dodger on that cold February day had given birth to a young one of her own. The mystery of life was an ongoing miracle. If only Elvis had lived!

★

Bizarrely, there were rumors that he *was* still alive. He'd been sighted everywhere . . . supermarkets, Burger Kings, and shopping malls. There was even a tape of what was alleged to be Elvis speaking, recorded after he was supposed to have died.

Various "proofs" are offered to support this belief that Elvis is alive.

The most important "evidence" that he is alive lies in the way his name is spelled, or rather misspelled, on his grave. According to the "misspelling theory," the misspelling on his grave "proves" that Elvis faked his own death. The grave reads Elvis *Aa*ron Presley, while Elvis most commonly spelled his middle name with only one *a*: Elvis *A*ron Presley. Therefore, by the logic of the misspelling theory, because the name is spelled wrong, Elvis cannot be in that grave.

Another argument centers on Lisa's behavior on the night that Elvis died. She played on her golf cart late into the evening, which is not a conventional way to respond to a father's death —"proving" that he couldn't really have died.

Finally, there is the tape that purports to be Elvis speaking after August 16, 1977.

Upon close examination, none of this "evidence" holds up.

Anyone who was familiar with Lisa would realize that nothing about her childhood was

★

conventional. They would also know how much that golf cart meant to her and her father. Driving around in circles on the night Elvis died, on the golf cart on which she and Elvis had played together so often, was Lisa's way of dealing with her grief.

As to the Elvis tape, one of the voice experts who identifies Elvis' voice misspells several words in his report: "basically" is spelled "basicly," "receiving" is spelled "recieving," and "through" is spelled "thru." Applying the misspelling theory, do these errors mean we can conclude the audio expert faked his own death?

And in fact, this lamebrained misspelling theory is not even applicable to Elvis' gravestone. It is true Elvis often used the *A*ron spelling for his middle name. "*A*ron" was the vernacular, phonetic spelling that his mother used at his birth.

But when his mother died, Elvis tried to legally change his middle name to the standard spelling—"*Aa*ron" with two *a*'s. He found, to his surprise, that on his official birth certificate his name was already spelled "*Aa*ron" and so he dropped the now unnecessary legal proceedings.

It turned out that when Elvis was born, the doctor who filled out the birth certificate spelled the middle name correctly. Elvis *Aa*ron Presley is the name on his birth certificate, Elvis *Aa*ron Presley is the name on his grave. The eighty

★

thousand fans who filed past the body in his open casket were not blind.

Elvis Presley is dead.

But Elvis lives!

For the entire world, he is still the legend he always was. His music will live on forever. He changed the course of rock 'n' roll history. For millions of fans, all that he gave them will never die.

But for Lisa, he is alive in another way—in her memories of him as a devoted father and as an example of how to be a generous, fully alive human being. Evidence of his love for her is still abundantly present. Graceland is hers, and hers alone. It is not Priscilla's, the bodyguards', the girlfriends', the stepbrother's, or the Colonel's. Nothing more clearly shows how Elvis' devotion to Lisa was unique, different from his affection for anyone else.

Graceland will always be there, looming at the end of the winding path beyond the music gates. Vernon and Dodger may be gone now. Mary Jenkins has retired. The swing set Lisa played on as a child outside Vernon's office is gently rusting away.

But Aunt Delta still waits inside Graceland with her little dog. Lisa slips in under cover of darkness, after the last tour is over.

As Lisa sits with Aunt Delta's dog, teasing it lightheartedly, it is almost like seeing Elvis

★

again. The resemblance between father and daughter grows more uncanny every day, not just in those famous features. For as Lisa plays with the dog and laughs in her jolly way, something of Elvis' personality comes across, too.

And now Lisa has brought forth a child, continuing Elvis' bloodline. One day Danielle will be told who her grandfather was. And on that day she will begin to share not just in Elvis' fortune, but in the memories he left behind.

Yes, Elvis does live . . . in Lisa, and in little baby Danielle!

ABOUT THE AUTHORS

DAVID ADLER is a writer who lives in Las Vegas.

ERNEST ANDREWS saw his first Elvis concert in 1955 in Chattanooga, Tennessee, and has been an Elvis fan ever since.

MEET THE SUPERSTARS
With St. Martin's Paperbacks!

ELVIS IN PRIVATE
Peter Haining, ed.
_____ 90902-0 $3.50 U.S.

McCARTNEY
Chris Salewicz
_____ 90451-7 $4.50 U.S.   _____ 90452-5 $5.50 Can.

HEMINGWAY
Christopher Cook Gilmore
_____ 91175-0 $3.50 U.S.   _____ 91176-9 $4.50 Can.

OPRAH!
Robert Waldron
_____ 91026-6 $3.50 U.S.   _____ 91027-4 $4.50 Can.

MERYL STREEP
Diana Maychick
_____ 90246-8 $3.50 U.S.   _____ 90248-4 $4.50 Can.

CHER
by J. Randy Taraborrelli
_____ 90849-0 $3.95 U.S.   _____ 90850-4 $4.95 Can.

Publishers Book and Audio Mailing Service
P.O. Box 120159, Staten Island, NY 10312-0004

Please send me the book(s) I have checked above. I am enclosing
_____ (please add $1.25 for the first book, and $.25 for each
additional book to cover postage and handling. Send check or
money order only—no CODs.)

Name _____

Address _____

City _____ State/Zip _____

Please allow six weeks for delivery. Prices subject to change
without notice.

STAR 1/89

PRISCILLA,
ELVIS
AND ME